Sex and the Sanctity of Human Life

The Truth of Catholic Teaching

William E. May

CHRISTENDOM PUBLICATIONS
Christendom College Press
Route 3, Box 87
Front Royal, Virginia 22630

L. C. Classification Number: HQ63.M28
ISBN: 0-931888-17-4

NIHIL OBSTAT:
    Rev. Edward J. Berbusse, S. J.
    Censor deputatus

IMPRIMATUR:
    †Most Rev. John R. Keating
    Bishop of Arlington
    May 25, 1984

To Leonard J. Keck

ACKNOWLEDGEMENTS

I am grateful to the editors and publishers of journals and books in which the essays found in this book were originally published. Ch. 1 appeared originally under the same title in *Catholic Faith and Human Life: Proceedings of the First Convention of the Fellowship of Catholic Scholars*, ed. George A. Kelly (New York: Fellowship of Catholic Scholars, 1979). It has been extensively rewritten for publication here. Ch. 2 was initially published as "The Logic of Love" in *Fidelity* 1.6 (May, 1982) and is here simply edited. Ch. 3 was first published in *Linacre Quarterly* 46 (1979) under the same title and is reprinted here with only minor changes. Ch. 4 originally appeared in the *Proceedings of the Thirty-Third Annual Convention, The Catholic Theological Society of America*, Vol. 33, ed. Luke Salm (Washington: Catholic Theological Society of America, 1979) under the same title. It has here been substantively rewritten and developed. Ch. 5 first appeared in *Faith & Reason* 3.1 (Spring, 1977) under the same title. It, too, has been extensively reworked. Ch. 6 originally appeared in *Homiletic and Pastoral Review* 82.4 (January, 1982) and appears essentially unchanged here. Ch. 7 was first published under the same title in *Homiletic and Pastoral Review* 77.11-12 (August-September, 1977). It has been very extensively reworked for publication here. Ch. 8 includes material published under the title, "Reverencing Human Life in Its Generation," in *New Technologies of Birth and Death* (St. Louis: Pope John XXIII Medical-Moral Research Center, 1980) and material published under the title "Artful Childmaking: Reproduction or Procreation?" in *Homiletic and Pastoral Review* 82.8 (May, 1982). Both have been modified and developed substantially for publication here.

CONTENTS

Introduction

This work is written with the firm conviction that the teaching of the Roman Catholic Church on human sexuality and sexual morality is rooted in a deep respect and reverence for the sanctity of human life. It is, moreover, a teaching that recognizes and takes seriously the *bodily* character of human existence and the centrality of free choice.

Today, however, the liberating truth of Catholic teaching is denied by many, including many Catholics and particularly by some influential theologians. Frequently the teaching of the Church is rejected in the name of personalism, and the charge is made that the "official" teaching of the Church is based on a narrow physicalism. I find this ironic, for when the issues are examined critically, as I hope to examine them in the chapters to follow, one discovers that the champions of the new personalism are the ones who are really physicalistic, for they fail to appreciate properly the bodily character of human personhood. Their personalism, as will become evident in the essays to follow, is in actuality an uncritical acceptance of a philosophy that ignores the deeper dimension of human life and limits the real and important simply to whatever may be occupying conscious thinking and living at the present moment. In addition, they do not, in my opinion, properly honor human freedom and our capacity to make or break our lives by our own free choices. Too frequently they allege that it is *impossible* for human persons to avoid contracepting or sterilizing or aborting or relieving their sexual tensions by masturbation, premarital and extramarital sex, and that therefore the choice to engage in these activities is the "best possible option" so long as "exploiting" others is avoided.

In the essays that follow two central issues emerge. These are dualism and moral methodology. The Church, through the firm, constant, and eloquent teachings of popes and councils, consistently maintains that human

7

persons, unlike the Divine Persons and angelic persons, are *bodily* persons and that their bodies are integrally personal. Thus, in the teaching of the Church, *every living human body is a person*, whether that living human body be unborn, newborn, mentally crippled, senile, or comatose and whether that body be male or female. As we shall see, revisionists who deny the teaching of the Church on moral issues frequently allege that some living human bodies, for instance, of unborn children, are not as yet "meaningfully" or "personally" alive; and the revisionists consistently maintain that the procreative dimension of our genital sexuality is, in and of itself, biological, with the need to be assumed into consciousness in order to be of personal and human significance.

The Church also consistently maintains with St. Paul in Romans 3.8 that it is *never* right to choose to do evil so that good may come about. Those who reject Church teaching on moral questions do so because in their judgment it is permissible to choose to do evil for the sake of greater good to come. They seek to support this claim by distinguishing between "premoral" (also called "nonmoral," "ontic," or "physical") evil and "moral" evil and by claiming that St. Paul's advice in Romans must be understood to mean that we are not to do *moral* evil so that good may come about. As we shall see in the chapters included here, this contention is erroneous.

The essays in this work have, for the most part, appeared originally in various journals and symposia. But in organizing them for publication in book form I have taken the opportunity to rework most of them quite substantively, in order to integrate into them in particular the thought of Pope John Paul II, to develop several themes, to take into account more recent literature, and, at times, to correct errors of my own, as will be noted in specific places. The specific questions of sexual morality with which these essays are concerned center on the problems of contraception and sterilization, with less consideration given to pre-marital and extra-marital genital sex. In addition, the final chapter of the work is specifically concerned with the laboratory generation of human life and abortion. While neither of these issues is itself specifically a question of sexual morality, both are intimately related to our understanding of ourselves as sexual, bodily persons. Since our differentiation into male and female is itself a matter quite illuminating about the character of our bodily existence, this subject is the focus of the first chapter.

Two years ago to the day, almost, on the feast of St. Augustine, I finished the manuscript of my *Sex, Marriage, and Chastity: Reflections of a Catholic Layman, Spouse, and Parent* (Chicago: Franciscan Herald Press, 1981). Today, on the feast of St. Augustine's mother, St. Monica, I finish this. Although there is some overlap in the matter taken up in each work, I believe that the two studies are complementary in nature. *Sex, Marriage, and Chastity* centers on the meaning of marriage as a human reality and Christian sacrament and the virtue of chastity, treating of contracpetion within the context of marriage. The present work, which deals more extensively with the issue of contraception and which takes up issues that were not discussed in the earlier volume (e.g., sterilization, the laboratory generation of life, abortion), is more directly concerned with the problem of moral methodology (particularly in chapter 5, 6, 7 and 8). Because of the need to make better known the authentic personalism at the heart of Catholic teaching and to call into question the dualistic personalism of its detractors, it is possible that a work of this kind may be of value. The leading ideas that it seeks to develop are by no means my own personal discovery; they have been mediated to me by the Catholic Church. All I seek to do is to explain this teaching as best I can and to offer what I hope are cogent criticisms of teachings at variance with it. May both St. Monica, the heroic wife and mother, and her son, St. Augustine, the great doctor of the Church, bless this work and all who read it. While it is popular today to disparage Augustine, particularly because of his views on sexuality, it is folly to do so. Although his thought was deficient in many ways, he searched the depths of the human person with a profundity hardly ever equalled, and from him we can learn much.

I wish to acknowledge the help and encouragement of many friends in the writing and rewriting of the essays found here, in particular the help of my wife, Patricia, of Rev. John F. Harvey, O.S.F.S., of Rev. Ronald Lawler, O.F.M. Cap., of Rev. William Smith, of Germain G. Grisez and Joseph M. Boyle, Jr. I also wish to acknowledge the debt I owe to our present pontiff, Pope John Paul II, for the stimulating and provocative presentation of Catholic teaching that he has made both in his writings as Karol Wojtyla (particularly in his *Love and Responsibility*) and in his papal addresses and in the Apostolic Exhortation, *Familiaris Consortio*. It is imperative, I believe, for the Catholic faithful and for all men and women of good will to become aware of his truly Christian personalism.

I dedicate this work to my father-in-law, Leonard J. Keck, who taught me much about the meaning of marital love in the care he gave so faithfully to my mother-in-law, Lucille Keck, in her long period of senility prior to death.

William E May
Feast of St. Monica
August 27, 1982

1.
Male and Female:
The Sexual Significance

Because human sexuality participates in the mystery of the human person, the last word on this subject can never be said. Moreover, precisely because it is so rich in intelligibility that its meaning can never be fully exhausted by any one person or group of persons, it is only reasonable to expect that there will be differences of opinion concerning it, differences that are not only complementary but, quite frequently, contradictory. Still this does not mean that we do not really know anything at all about the meaning of human sexuality.[1] My purpose here will be to develop an understanding of human sexuality and of the significance of the fact that the human species is sexually differentiated into male and female. This understanding is, in my judgment, true; and while it is open to ever deeper and richer development, its truth is of critical importance to human persons and human societies.

Before reflecting on the meaning of human sexuality, however, I want to make some brief observations about the significance of being human and to show why a grasp of what it means to be human is centrally important in evaluating *any* understanding of human sexuality.

To be a human being is to be, first and foremost, a being of moral worth or person, a bearer of transcendent value, the subject of a dignity and a sanctity that ought to be recognized by others and protected by society. This proposition, I believe, can be defended philosophically on the grounds that a human being, i.e., a living member of the human species, is a being radically different in kind from other kinds of living beings of which we have experience, and that membership in this species is, therefore, of crucial moral significance, conferring a status on a human being that is not enjoyed by other beings that we know.[2] Religiously, this proposition is rooted in the belief that a human being is a living image or icon of God Himself, a "word" uttered by God, the created "word" that His Uncreated Word became.

All human beings are by virtue of their membership in the human species beings of moral worth or "persons."[3] Included in this species are many who are *not* consciously aware of themselves and capable of relating to other selves in a "meaningful" way. Still all of these human beings are beings of moral worth, "persons," and as such equal in dignity and value.

To be human, then, is to be a person. But the human person is not a spirit person; it is a *bodied* person, an animal person. A human person is a living human body, and so long as we have within our midst a living human body we have present to us an irreplaceable, priceless human person. The developing living human body within a pregnant woman is a person, not a mass of genetic materials; a comatose, but still living human body, is a person, not a "living vegetable."

Since human persons are body persons, they are inevitably sexual persons. In creating human persons, God created a biological species of a unique kind, but a species sexually differentiated into male and female. To be a human person, therefore, is to be a sexual being. There are no asexual members of the human species; rather all of us are either male or female. I believe that any true understanding of human sexuality must take seriously the bodily character of our personhood, recognizing that our bodies are not subpersonal tools of a "conscious subject" distinct from them but are rather integrally personal dimensions of our existence.[4]

"Sexuality," Pope John Paul II reminds us, "is by no means something purely biological, but concerns the innermost being of the human person as such.[5] The fact that one human person is a *male* and that another is a *female* is not something merely incidental to their being, a matter of sheer facticity, a purely biological "given" that the person is called upon to "transcend."[6] *Maleness* and *femaleness* are not mere anatomical differences but are different modes of *being* human. A man and a woman are different not only anatomically and culturally but psychically and ontologically. One contemporary writer, Mary Rosera Joyce, puts it this way:

> Man and woman are different in the very depths of their existence. Their more apparent anatomical differences are not . . . mere attachments to their common human nature; differences in the body are *revelations* of differences in the depths of their beings. . . . The idea that sex is biological only is a serious affront to the unity of the human person.[7]

Another contemporary, Pope John Paul II, expresses this by saying that male and female "are, as it were, two 'incarnations' of the same metaphysical solitude/that man, male and female, is as a unique being in creation/ before God and the world—*two ways, as it were, of 'being a body' and at the same time a man, which complete each other.*"[8]

This truth about human persons, although difficult to express clearly and unambiguously, is crucial, for it shows that human persons are not sexless intelligences but are rather irreplaceable and unrepeatable men and women of flesh and blood. A human person is not an immaterial substance or subjectivity that simply happens, as the authors of the CTSA report on human sexuality put it, to be "embodied in *either* a male *or* a female body-structure."[9] Rather a human person is a bodily being whose person is that of a male or female, a sexual being.

Men and women, therefore, differ not only physically and anatomically but metaphysically. They sense differently, they feel differently, they think differently, they love differently.[10] This deeply rooted difference between male and female is perhaps the reason, as George Gilder, Stephen Clark, Lucius Cervantes and others have so richly documented,[11] why a woman more easily discovers her sexual identity in being herself and why a man must go out of himself in deeds to establish his sexual identity.

It is particularly important to realize that our sexuality is not to be identified with our sexual organs. Our sexual organs are indeed integrally personal and are not simply tools that persons use, now for one purpose and now for another.[12] Still, these organs, though revelatory of our being as men and women, do not exhaust our sexuality, our maleness and femaleness. Our sexuality, in other words, is not only genital but is a modality or dimension of our existence as sentient, affective, body persons who are capable of coming into possession of ourselves as sexual beings through acts of understanding and of love.

What this means is that sexuality—and with it our sexual desires and powers—is not in and of itself integrative. Rather it needs to be integrated within ourselves by the virtue of chastity, which Pope John Paul II describes as precisely the aptitude to master the movements of sexual desire or concupiscence, so that we can thereby come into possession of ourselves as sexual beings and not become possessed by desire.[13] A human person is capable of becoming fully himself without expressing himself in acts of genital coition. It is not, in short, necessary to experience orgasm in order to be fully male or fully female.[14]

The claims made in the foregoing paragraphs are, in my judgment, true. Yet they need to be substantiated, and the evidence in support of them needs to be marshalled and developed. This I hope to do in the following reflections.

One of the most important sexual differences is that the male can never become pregnant (and knows so), whereas the female can (and knows so), and she can become pregnant not by taking thought but by taking into her body the body person of the male and receiving from him his seed. At the same time, one of the most important similarities between the male and the female is that they both need to touch others and to be touched by others. They need to do so because they are body persons. They also dread offensive touches, invasions of their privacy, violations of their body person. They can reach out and touch others in many different ways, but there is one sort of touch that is unique and by its very nature bears on differences between male and female, and this is the touch of genital coition.

This is a unique sort of touch for two special reasons. It is unique, first, because it involves a way of touching significantly different for the male and the female. She can not, in the act of genital coition enter into the person of the male, whereas he can personally enter into her, and she is uniquely capable of receiving him. What this indicates, as Robert Joyce has noted, is that in the male sexuality is a giving in a receiving sort of way, whereas in the female sexuality is a receiving in a giving sort of way.[15] This way of touching is unique, second, because it can and sometimes does lead to the female's becoming pregnant, a bearer of a new human life.[16] This touch, in short, is unique because it is unitive and procreative.

The facts noted in the foregoing paragraph support the view that human sexuality includes, somewhat differently for each sex, affective and genital dimensions. These two dimensions are inseparably linked in the *one* human person, a sexual being who is either male or female. Moreover, the genital component is both a way of being affectionate (unitive) and the only way in which males and females can be life-giving (procreative).[17]

Today many people believe that the fundamental *human* and *personal* significance of our sexuality is its affective component, in particular its coital-genital union, and that its procreative component is simply a biological function. These people, among them a number of prominent theologians, propose therefore an ideology of affectionate, relational, creatively interpersonal, and nonprocreative sex.[18] Their understanding of human sexuality can properly be called "separatist," for they sever the bonds between the unitive/amative/affectionate dimension of human sexuality and its procreative dimension, deeming the former alone as personal and human and the latter as merely a biological function, of itself subpersonal in character and of human and personal significance only when consciously willed and chosen.[19]

In company with many others, including George Gilder, Paul Ramsey, and, significantly, Popes Paul VI and John Paul II,[20] I believe that this separatist ideology is a serious misunderstanding of the significance of our existence as sexual persons. There is something of paramount human significance in the fact that one special kind of touch, the touch of coital sex, not only requires for its exercise a difference between male and female but also expresses in its own inherent dynamism an intimate, exclusive sharing of life and love. Moreover, this touch, open to the transmission of life, is capable of communicating that life and that love to a new human being, a new body person of priceless and irreplaceable value.

The generating of a new human life is not an act comparable to the making of a table or a car; it is not an act of "reproduction"—as many of the advocates of the separatist understanding prefer to call it—and it is not this sort of an act because a human person is *not* a product inferior to its producers but rather is a being equal in dignity to and one in nature with its parents. A human person is the image or word of God, and like the Uncreated Word a human person is to be begotten, not made. Furthermore, the newly formed and developing human person is one of the most helpless and dependent of all beings. The best way—God's plan for human beings, as the Church has consistently taught[21]—to provide this new human person with the love it needs to develop the powers it possesses is to give it a mother and a father who are willing to share their life and love with a being who comes into existence through the same act whereby they express their own deep, intimate, and exclusive love for one another.

Thus, despite the current ideology of nonprocreative relational sex, we find that sex takes on a new centrality and depth in relation to our capacity to share life with a new generation of human persons. Our power to do this, our procreative power, is thus by no means subpersonal or subhuman, a mere biological function. It is, rather, a significant human or personal power inherently and intimately linked to our very being.[22] As Pope John Paul II has put it, human fertility "is directed to the generation of a human being, and so by its nature it surpasses the purely biological order and involves a whole series of personal values."[23]

It is now necessary to examine more closely the significance of our sexuality as affectionate, passionate beings, who long to touch and be touched by others. Among the ways in which we can touch another person, the genital sexual touch is, as we have already seen, unique. In and through it, the man and the woman are able to manifest what John Paul II has termed the "nuptial meaning of the body," that is, its meaning as a gift from God, an expression of His life and love and a reality that is, of itself, open to life.[24] It is, moreover, not just any kind of life and love that is meant to be shared through this deeply personal deed; through this act each comes to "know" the other and to be "known" by that other in a unique way. The kind of love meant to be expressed by this sexual touch is aptly called "spousal" or "wedded" love, a love different in kind from ordinary friendship love, the kind of love we are meant to extend to all.

This love, so richly described in *Gaudium et Spes*, the Pastoral Constitution on the Modern World of Vatican II, in Pope Paul VI's encyclical *Humanae vitae*, and in the writings of Pope John Paul II both prior to and subsequent to his election as Pope,[25] will be taken up at more length in Chapter 3, below. Here I would like to note how this love is analyzed by the philosopher Dietrich von Hildebrand and by the psychologist Erich Fromm. Von Hildebrand says that spousal love "aspires to a union which extends much further than that of simple friendship, filial love, or parental love. It desires bodily union. . . . Spousal love aspires to the bodily union as a specific fulfillment of the total union, as a unique, deep, mutual self-donation."[26] Spousal love, obviously, is the kind of love intended to characterize the love between man and woman in marriage, the kind of love symbolizing and inwardly participating in the love of Christ for His bride, the Church.

It is important to note, however, that Von Hildebrand says that spousal love "aspires to" a unique and total self-donation. He recognized that spousal love, as an aspiration or desire, can and does arise in persons who are not married, and who, possibly, can never become married because of tragic circumstances. His point is that spousal love is the kind of love that is ordered to marriage, promised in marriage, and meant to characterize marriage. Indeed, as we shall see in Chapter 4, it is marriage itself that makes spousal love, as an actuality and not merely as an aspiration and desire, possible.

It is instructive, in my opinion, to note that this notion of spousal love, seems to be precisely the type of love to which the psychologist Erich Fromm refers when he speaks of "erotic" love and distinguishes it from all other kinds of love. For Fromm erotic love is a distinct type of friendship love and its difference arises from its *exclusive* character, a character that needs to be carefully and properly understood. The exclusivity of erotic love is by no means a type of jealous possessiveness, nor does it mean that erotic or spousal love for one particular, unique person excludes warmth, affection, and friendship love for others. Fromm puts it this way:

> In erotic love there is an exclusiveness that is lacking in brotherly love and motherly love. The exclusive character of erotic love warrants further discussion. Frequently the exclusiveness of erotic love is misrepresented as meaning possessive attachment. One can find two

people "in love" with each other who feel no love for anybody else. Their love is, in fact, an *égoism à deux*. . . . They have the experience of overcoming aloneness yet, since they are separated from the rest of mankind, they remain separated from each other and alienated from themselves; their experience of union is an illusion. Erotic love is exclusive, but it loves in the other person all of mankind, all that is alive. It is exclusive in the sense that I can fuse myself fully and intensely with one person alone. Erotic love excludes the love of others only in the sense of erotic fusion, full commitment in all aspects of life—but not in the sense of deep brotherly love.[27]

There is, then, a very special kind of human love, one that is thematically sexual in character, aptly termed "spousal" or "conjugal" love. It is *this* kind of love, one that is exclusive yet nonpossessive, that gives human significance to the genital sexual touch, to the act of human coition. It is important to see why.

Earlier I stressed that our sexuality includes both affective and genital components—and in saying this there was no intent to sever the two; far from it, for the genital dimension of our sexuality is intended to be an exceptionally intimate mode of expressing affection, of touching and being touched by another human person. As males and females, we can reach out in friendship to touch all of the persons with whom we live. But, as men and women who lovingly and intelligently order our lives, we are to reach out and to touch in genital sexuality only that person with whom we will share conjugal or spousal love. There are many reasons why this is true and why this truth has much to tell us about ourselves and our existence as sexual beings; I shall now attempt to explore some of these reasons.

We body persons are unique among the living beings of our experience not only in our capacity to share and communicate life and love to others but also in our vulnerability and in our ability to wound others. We are the most woundable of animals, and in sharing our person (and this is precisely what we *are* doing in acts of coition, of genital touching) we are exchanging vulnerabilities, we are risking our lives—and we are risking the life of the person with whom we are sharing our own.

Life entails risks, of course; but the person who seeks to come into possession of himself and to integrate his sexual humanity does not risk his life or the life of another irreplaceably precious human person wantonly. We are, in brief, to come into possession of ourselves and not let ourselves become possessed by our desires. And precisely because of our vulnerability we should choose to touch another and to be touched by another in the act of genital coition only when, together, we are ready to share spousal love;

for it is only this kind of love that rightly respects the intrinsic worth, the unique irreplaceability, and vulnerability of the human person.

I realize that at times there may be tender and affectionate acts of genital coition between persons who are unable to give each other spousal love. Fornication need not be brutal. Nonetheless the tenderness and affection present are so not because those engaging in such actions are unmarried, but despite the fact. And there *is* present an element of tragedy, of poignant sadness, and this precisely because something of crucial human significance that ought to be present is missing: the ability to give spousal love, an ability that is made possible only by the covenant of marriage. But because of this the action in question is deprived of what ought to be integral to it, and this deprivation of the good that ought to be present makes it evil. *Bonum ex integra causa, malum ex quocumque defectu.*

Moreover, and this is something that cannot be concealed from the human mind, even in this contraceptive age, genital coition *is* genital: that is, it possesses a procreative dimension, one rooted in the procreative sexuality of male and female. The act whereby a man and a woman can express and are meant to express in a unique way the special kind of friendship known as spousal love is an act that is open to the transmission of life. It is an act that of its own inner dynamism is open to the generation of a new human person, a child who has the right to be wanted, to be touched, to be given a home where he can take root and to be loved. The affective/unitive and genital/procreative dimension of human sexuality are, as Pope Paul VI stressed in *Humanae vitae*, inseparably connected.[28]

The touch of genital sexuality, the *sex act*, is a touch that is meant to participate in the love-giving and life-giving covenant of God's awesome plan for Man, whom He created "male and female." The touch of genital coition is fitting, appropriate, and of truly human significance only within the covenant of marriage, a human reality inwardly receptive to the covenant of God's grace, a reality that has indeed been integrated into this convenant by the redemptive death and resurrection of Christ. Within the reality of marriage, which is, as the Fathers of Vatican II teach, "rooted in the conjugal covenant of irrevocable personal consent" and an image of and particpation in "the loving covenant uniting Christ with the Church,"[29] this touch itself becomes a covenantal and sacramental reality.

Everything said in this chapter is summarzied by Pope John Paul II in *Familiaris Consortio*, and it is fitting to conclude this chapter with this passage from his inspiring apostolic exhortation:

> Sexuality, by means of which man and woman give themselves to one another through the acts which are proper and exclusive to spouses,

is by no means something purely biological, but concerns the innermost being of the human person as such. It is realized in a truly human way only if it is an integral part of the love by which a man and a woman commit themselves totally to one another until death. The total physical self-giving would be a lie if it were not the sign and fruit of a total personal self-giving, in which the whole person, including the temporal dimension, is present: If the person were to withhold something or reserve the possibility of deciding otherwise in the future, by the very fact he or she would not be giving totally.

This totality which is required by conjugal love also corresponds to the demands of responsible fertility. This fertility is directed to the generation of a human being, and so by its nature it surpasses the purely biological order and involves a whole series of personal values. . . .

The only "place" in which this self-giving in its whole truth is made possible is marriage, the covenant of conjugal love freely and consciously chosen, whereby man and woman accept the intimate community of life and love willed by God himself, which only in this light manifests its true meaning. The institution of marriage is not an undue interference by society or authority, nor the extrinsic imposition of a form. Rather it is an interior requirement of the covenant of conjugal love which is publicly affirmed as unique and exclusive in order to live in complete fidelity to the plan of God, the creator.[30]

NOTES

[1] On this question see the development by Bernard Lonergan of the distinction between categorical and transcendental questions and of the movement, within the human person, from experience to understanding to critical reflection and responsible action. His thought on this matter is briefly summarized in the first chapter of his *Method in Theology* (New York: Herder and Herder, 1972).

[2] See the important book by Mortimer Adler, *The Difference of Man and the Difference it Makes* (New York: Meridian Books, 1968).

[3] The term "person" is a philosophical one, and many contemporaries use it in the sense of an entity aware of itself as a self (e.g., Michael Tooley, "Abortion and Infanticide," *Philosophy & Public Affairs* 2 (1972) 37-65. Such an understanding of "person" excludes a great number of human beings. The term in its Boethian sense, namely as an individual of a rational nature, is applicable to all members of the human species. In the sense of a "being of moral worth," person is, in Christian faith and, in my judgment, in philosphical truth, a predicate of *all* members of the human species. For a good philosophical study of "person" and of the reasons why all human beings, including tiny unborn ones, are persons and must be recognized as such, see Robert Joyce, "When Does a Person Begin?" in *New Perspectives on Abortion*, ed. Thomas Hilgers, David Horan,

and David Mall (Lanham, Md.: University Press of America, 1981), pp. 345-346.

⁴ Pope John Paul II has developed, both as pope, and prior to his election as pontiff, as Karol Wojtyla, a magnificent understanding of the human person as a bodily being. See in particular his *The Acting Person* (Boston: Riedel, 1979) and his Wednesday conferences on the body, sex, and marriage. The first cycle of his talks on this subject have been published under the title *The Original Unity of Man and Woman: Catechesis on Genesis* (Boston: St. Paul Publications, 1981). A fine summary of his three cycles of addresses on this subject is provided by Richard M. Hogan, "A Theology of the Body," *Fidelity* 1.1. (December, 1981) 10-15, 24-27. The integral humanism of Pope John Paul II, like that of St. Thomas Aquinas, is in striking contrast to the dualistic view of man so common today, one that separates the person from the body and regards persons simply as conscious subjectivities attached to bodies.

⁵ Pope John Paul II, *Familiaris Consortio*, n. 11.

⁶ The attitude that sex is simply bodily and that the body is subhuman, a matter of sheer facticity, is, of course, Gnostic and Manichean in its roots. It is, despite all the talk about the centrality of sex and the reality of the body, the view evidenced in the report, *Human Sexuality: New Directions in American Catholic Thought* by Anthony Kosnik et al. (New York: Paulist, 1977). See in particular p. 84, where the authors of this work speak of the facticity of our bodily structure, a facticity that we, i.e. the personal subjects, are to transcend. For further criticism of this view, so widespread in our culture, see the booklet I co-authored with John Harvey, O.S.F.S., *On Understanding "Human Sexuality"* (Chicago: Franciscan Herald Press, 1977); see also Chapter One of my *Sex, Marriage, and Chastity: Reflections of a Catholic Layman, Spouse, and Parent* (Chicago: Franciscan Herald Press, 1981).

⁷ Mary Rosera Joyce, in the book co-authored with her husband, Robert, *New Dynamics of Sexual Love* (Collegeville, Mn.: St. John's University Press, 1970), pp. 34-35. Although I agree with the Joyces that sexuality is a being-ful difference and is by no means simply anatomical or even psychological, I believe that it is rooted in our being as corporeal, bodily entities who must touch others physically in order to communicate and share life. If we were to use Aristotelian categories, I would suggest that sexuality is an entitative habit, modifying the entire being of male and female. Male and female are not, of course, different *species*, but their differences are entitative in that they permeate their being. I fear that the Joyces' view, if pushed, would make male and female *different in species*. Despite my concern over this aspect of their work, I believe that their phenomenological analyses of the differences between male and female are superbly insightful and of tremendous value. Robert Joyce has further developed the ideas he and his wife set forth in this book in his *Human Sexual Ecology* (Washington, D.C.: University Press of America, 1980).

⁸ Pope John Paul II, "Marriage: One and Indissoluble in Genesis," in *The Original Unity of Man and Woman*, p. 79.

⁹ Kosnik et al., p. 84.

[10] On this question see the following: Stephen C. Clark, *Man and Woman in Christ* (Ann Arbor: Servant Books, 1980), in particular the initial chapter of Part Two; Ruth Tiffany Barnhouse, "Male and Female Sexuality Compared," in her *Homosexuality: A Symbolic Confusion* (New York: Seabury, 1977), pp. 62-76, and her essay, "On the Differences Between Men and Woman," in *Male and Female: Christian Approaches to Sexuality*, ed. Ruth Tiffany Barnouse and Urban T. Holmes, III (New York: Seabury, 1976), pp. 3-16.

[11] See George Gilder, *Sexual Suicide* (New York: Quadrangle Books, 1973; reprint, New York: Signet, 1975), in particular chapters 1 and 2. See also Carle Zimmermann and Lucius F. Cervantes, *Marriage and the Family: A Text for Moderns* (Chicago: Henry Regnery, 1956), pp. 137-292 (By Cervantes). It is interesting to note the similarity between the debates going on today and those that took place in the late 1940's and 1950's about the differences between men and women. On reading Cervantes (published in 1956) and then on reading Gilder (who is reacting to the rhetoric of such militant feminists as Germaine Greer, Susan Brownmiller et al.) and also in reading Clark (see note 10) (who is reacting to the claims of Rosemary Reuther, Elisabeth Schüssler Fiorenza et al.) one has the experience of *deja vu*.

[12] This is the view definitely set forth by Joseph Fletcher. See in particular p. 211 of his *Morals and Medicine* (Boston: Beacon Press, 1960). It is also the view set forth, in my judgment, in the so-called majority report of the papal commission on the regulation of births. See the text of this report in *The Birth-Control Debate*, ed. Robert Hoyt (Kansas City: National Catholic Reporter, 1968) and the critique of this report in my *Sex, Love, and Procreation* (Chicago: Franciscan Herald Press, 1976).

[13] For discussion of the virtue of chastity see Karol Wojtyla (Pope John Paul II), *Love and Responsibility* (New York: Farra, Straus, Giroux, 1981), pp. 143-173; also my *The Nature and Meaning of Chastity* (Chicago: Franciscan Herald Press, 1976); and Albert Plé, O.P., *Chastity and the Affective Life* (New York: Herder and Herder, 1965), truly a superb work.

[14] It ought to be evident, I believe, that our Lord Jesus Christ was a fully sexed male and that His Blessed Mother was a fully sexed female.

[15] On this see Robert Joyce, *Human Sexual Ecology*, Chapter 5.

[16] For a development of this idea see below, Chapter 8.

[17] It remains true to say that human procreativity is possible only through the *spousal* touch of sexual coition even in this age of artificial insemination, in vitro fertilization, etc. As will be shown in a later chapter, when married persons engage in in vitro fertilization and other modes of laboratory generation of human life their capacity to do so is not rooted in their being as spouses but simply in the fact that they are producers of gametic cells. Such generation of human life is not a procreative act but is rather one of reproduction.

[18] Exponents of this view include, among others, the following: Michael Valente, *Sex: The Radical View of a Catholic Theologian* (New York: Bruce, 1970); Robert and Anna Francoeur, "The Ethics of Man Made Sex," in *The*

Future of Sexual Relations, ed. Robert and Anna Francoeur (Englewood Cliffs, N.J.: Prentice-Hall, 1973); Kosnik et al., *Human Sexuality*; John McNeill, *The Church and the Homosexual* (Kansas City: Sheed, Ward, McMeel, 1977). A very sophisticated and urbane presentation of this view so widespread today, is given by Ashley Montagu in the first chapter of his *Sex, Man, and Culture* (Philadelphia: Lippincott, 1969).

[19] For further criticism of this view see Chapter One of my *Sex, Marriage, and Chastity*.

[20] Pope Paul VI, *Humanae vitae*; Pope John Paul II, *Familiaris Consortio*, nn. 28-35; Gilder, *Sexual Suicide*, Chapters One and Two; Paul Ramsey, *Fabricated Man* (New Haven: Yale University Press, 1971), Chapter One. While Professor Ramsey is clearly opposed to the dualistic, separatistic understanding of human sexuality, he does, unfortunately, accept contraception. He uses an argument similar to one of the arguments developed by the authors of the "majority report," namely, the distinction between the marriage as a whole and individual acts within the marriage, an argument that is quite specious. For a critique of this argument see Chapter Four of my *Sex, Marriage and Chastity*. Nonetheless, Ramsey definitely rejects and submits to penetrating criticism the dualism and separatism so dominant today and reflected in the works cited in note 18.

[21] It is always to *God's plan* that the Church refers in speaking of marriage and the sexual order. This is constantly reaffirmed in the magisterial documents and runs like a refrain through Pope Pius XI's *Casti Connubii*, the paragraphs devoted to marriage in *Gaudium et Spes*, Pope Paul VI's *Humanae vitae*, and Pope John Paul II's *Familiaris Consortio*.

[22] For a development of this idea, see below, Chapter 3, "Fertility Awareness and Sexuality."

[23]*Familiaris Consortio* n. 11.

[24] On this see in particular Pope John Paul II's Address of January 9, 1980, "The Nuptial Meaning of the Body," in *the Original Unity of Man and Woman*, pp. 106-112.

[25] *Gaudium et Spes*, nn. 49-50; Pope Paul VI, *Humanae vitae* n. 9; Karol Wojtyla (Pope John Paul II), *Love and Responsibility* pp. 73-100; *Familiaris Consortio*, nn. 18-27.

[26] Dietrich von Hildebrand, *Man and Woman* (Chicago: Franciscn Herald Press, 1965), p. 18.

[27] Erich Fromm, *The Art of Loving* (New York: Harper and Row, 1965), p. 55.

[28] Pope Paul VI, *Humanae vitae*, no. 13.

[29] *Gaudium et Spes*, nn. 49-52..

[30] *Familiaris Consortio*, n. 11.

2.
The Liberating Truth of Catholic Teaching on Sexual Morality: The Logic of Love

In order to appreciate the truth and beauty of the Church's teaching on sexual morality it is first necessary to put it into its proper context: the Church's teaching on the meaning of human existence in the light of Divine Revelation.

Our moral life can, I think, be described as an endeavor first, on the *cognitive* level, to come *to know* who we are and what we are to do if we are to be the beings we are meant to be and second, on the *conative* level, *to do* what we come to know we are to do. Thus an understanding of the Church's teaching about *who we are* and *what we are to be* provides the indispensable context for grasping the truth of its teaching about what we are to do.

As we have already seen, the Church, in proclaiming the gospel and communicating to us the saving truth of God's revealing word, teaches that each human being is an irreplaceable, priceless person, a being of moral worth. Of each of us has it been written, "Does a woman forget her baby at the breast, or fail to cherish the son of her womb? Yet even if they forget, I will never forget you. See, I have branded your name on the palms of my hands" (Is 49.15-16). Every human being is a living image of God Himself, an icon or living representative of the all-holy and all-loving God. Every one of us is, as it were, a "word" uttered by God Himself; in fact, each one of us is the "created word" of God that His Uncreated Word became (Jn 1.1, 14) precisely to show us how deeply God loves us and cherishes us as irreplaceable and precious persons.

Every human being, moreover, is called to a life of friendship with God Himself. God made us to be the kind of beings capable of sharing His own inner life, and to enable us actually to receive this life God Himself became, in the person of His only begotten Son, one with us and for us. He took upon Himself our humanity—a humanity that had, because of original sin, been wounded and rendered impotent even of receiving the gift for which it had, by God's grace, been originally created—precisely so that we might be actually capable of participating in His own Divine life. In and through baptism we actually become children of God Himself, members of His family, with the right to call Him, in union with His only begotten Son Jesus Christ, "Abba," "Father." Thus we are *to be* His children, intimate members of His Divine family, alive with His own life. This life begins in us in baptism, and it is to be fulfilled in the resurrection, when we become fully the persons we are meant to be. Thus it is that the Risen Lord Jesus *is now* the human being *we* are to be. He is the "first fruits of the dead," living now the life to which we are called and for which we are capacitated, because of Him who is "our best and wisest friend."[1]

This teaching of the Church is significant here, because it means that any theory of human sexuality must be one in which *all* members of the human species (all living human bodies, all persons), are recognized as the beings that they are, that is, beings of moral worth, of irreplaceable value, summoned to be living members of God's Divine family.

As bodily persons[2] we both need to and long to touch others and to be touched by them—in a human, warm, loving way, of course—and we dread "offensive" touches because of the terrible wounds that they can inflict upon us. It is by touching and by being touched that we first come into conscious awareness of ourselves and of other persons (imagine how difficult it would be for a baby who is never touched and never allowed to touch others to develop!)

The pleasures and delights, the pains and sufferings that can be experienced by us include, of course, those that far surpass anything tactilely or sensibly experienceable. We know too that union with God, a union that is both a Divine gift and a result of acts of understanding and of love, is the happiness for which we most deeply yearn and for which we have been created. Nonetheless, as bodily persons we begin our journey home to Him—the Father, Son, and Spirit who loves us so deeply that He has become indissolubly one with us in Jesus—in fellowship with other bodily persons whom we come to know first, although by no means last and best, through bodily contact, through touching. Indeed, it is by the "touch" of baptismal water that we first enter into the Divine family.

Our need—and our vulnerability—as bodily persons to touch others and to be touched by them is intimately related to our being as sexual persons. Sex and touch are so closely interrelated that we can in truth speak of sexual affectivity. Sex is so deeply rooted in our being as bodily persons[3] that it extends beyond our gential sexuality to include and permeate our whole emotional and affective life.

Sex, thus, is central to our lives and is deeply rooted in our being precisely because we are bodily persons. Our sexuality and our nature as sentient, feeling, emotional beings are not "subpersonal" or "brutal'" dimensions of our existence. To reach out to other persons and to develop the ability to understand and love them is first of all made possible for us as bodily persons because we are intelligent, sentient, and sexual beings. We have sexual longings and a need to touch and to be touched because we are bodily persons.

Our task is to learn how to touch (and allow ourselves to be touched) rightly, humanly, with reverence for the irreplaceable preciousness of the human person. We need to learn how to touch "lovingly." How, then, is love related to touch, and in particular to the genital/coital touch? To understand how, we need first to reflect briefly on the meaning of "love."[4]

Love, of course, is a many splendored thing, and the term is used (and abused) in a wide variety of ways. One sometimes wonders whether it is possible to determine its meaning at all or to say anything truthful about it, so widely is it used. We say that we love a poem or a sunset or our children or a hot-fudge sundae. We experience love as something that we do and also as something that comes over us and happens to us. We speak of God's love for us and even say that God *is* love. There is, thus, a need to sort out the various meanings of love and to distinguish its varied forms.

Yet before attempting this it is important to see the unity in love's varied forms. Language itself, testifying to something deep in human experience, resists efforts to sever all connections between a specific form of love and just plain love, for instance the effort to substitute uniformly "charity" or *caritas* or *agape* to designate God's love for us for "love." As Josef Pieper notes

> . . . in German and in other languages as well a single fundamental word apparently underlies all the variety in vocabulary and binds together all special meanings. In Latin, for example, and in all modern languages derived from it, this fundamental word is *amor*. "All gift

love or *caritas* is love, but not all love is gift love or *caritas*''; this sentence (taken from Thomas Aquinas) simply confirms existing usage; that all *dilectio* . . . and all *caritas* . . . is fundamentally *amor*.[5]

Yet what can the unity underlying the various forms of love be? With Pieper and others let me suggest that ''in every conceivable case love signifies much the same as approval. This is first of all to be taken in the literal sense of the word's root: loving someone or something means finding him or it *probus*, one Latin word for good. . . . It is a way of turning to him or it and saying, 'it is good that you exist.' ''[6] Basically, then, love means an affirmation of existence, and there is splendid reason for this. Surely it is true that ''the most marvelous of all things a being can do is to be.'' Existence itself, moreover, is a gift from God, an expression of *His* love. And seemingly we human beings require over and above sheer existence to be loved by other persons and to love them in order fully to be the beings God wills us to be.

Love thus basically means an affirmation of existence, of being. As something we do or practice it is a willingness to be and to let be in all fullness—as Pope John Paul II has noted again and again[7]—and, as something that we experience, that comes over us like an enchantment, it is the experience of a conferral of being upon ourselves. And as leading us to interpersonal communion, as a making-one or an act of atonement, it is friendship, the *amor amicitiae*. When we love another person and are in turn loved by him we not only affirm his being but enter into communion and fellowship with him, and in so doing come into a new possession of ourselves.

In the love of friendship we need affirm the existence of the person whom we love. How strange, indeed absurd, would it be for a friend to say of his friend that he wills his non-existence! Still friendship love is not an undifferentiated approval of everything that the friend is or does. It is not a thoughtless acceptance of his givenness here and now. Friendship love, precisely because it is *love* and thus an affirmation of the fullness of being, is a demanding, challenging love. We will our friend to be fully what he is meant to be; precisely because of our love of him we want him to rid himself of his failings, to discover his true needs and struggle for their attainment, and we are ready to help him in his struggle.

Authentic human friendship moreover, is the sort of love that is inwardly open to the Divine love (*agape, caritas*) that God wills to pour into our hearts if we but let Him. Like all love, this Divine love affirms existence and wills the fullness of being for the beloved. But this is a love that is not only a *response* to a loveableness that is already present, it is even more a love that is *creative* of goodness and loveableness and *redemptive* of goodness that has been impaired or disfigured. This Divine love, which prompted the Eternal, Uncreated Word of God to empty Himself and to become as we are and even to suffer death on the cross (cf. Phil 2:6-8), is a sacrificial kind of love. It is the kind of love that a person has if he is willing to give up his own claims and legitimate interests, even to give up his own life. It is by no means a doormat love, a pseudo-love that would repudiate justice and the reverence we are to have for ourselves and others as beings made in the image of God, but it is the kind of love that is ready, when necessary, to suffer injustice and to be sacrificial. It is the kind of love that is unwilling to do evil, even when the willingness to do evil is ordered to the achievement of some good (cf. Romans 3:8); rather it is ready to suffer evil rather than to do evil.[9]

We must, therefore, learn to love—that is, to will what is good and to reverence the irreplaceable preciousness of every human person, every living image of the all-holy God—if we are to touch others, and allow ourselves to be touched by them, lovingly.

Among the myriad ways in which we can touch another one of unique significance is the genital/coital touch, as we have seen. It is unique because it is a person-uniting touch, one that makes two persons to be "one flesh." As a person-uniting touch, genital/coital sex is, moreover, one that marvelously illuminates the complementary difference of male and female and, for husband and wife, this touch is supremely unitive because they have already, by their act of irrevocable choice, made each other to be irreplaceable and nonsubstitutable persons in each other's lives.[10] Their marriage makes them *to be* irreplaceable and non-substitutable.[11] Precisely because they *are* already spouses, they are capable of giving to one another spousal or conjugal love, the unique, exclusive kind of human love that "merges the human with the divine."[12]

When nonmarried individuals choose to touch one another in this way, they show that they do not understand the significance of love or the *person-uniting* meaning of the genital/coital touch. For their sexual union does *not* unite two irreplaceable and non-substitutable persons; rather it couples *two replaceable and substitutable individuals*. These individuals falsify the significance of this touch and show that what they love is not the irreplaceable person of the other but rather the benefit they gain from another individual, one who is in principle treated as a thing, a replaceable and substitutable object.[13]

The genital/coital touch is also a unique way of touching because it is life-giving. Since the male is continuously fertile from puberty until death (unless there is some pathological ailment), he knows—or ought to know—

that whenever he chooses to touch a woman in this way he can generate a new human life and cause the woman to be "with child." Today, of course, because of *contra*-ceptives, *anti*-procreative means, individuals can choose to repudiate the significance of this touch as a life-giving one, but this choice is hardly a choice of a loving person, of one who affirms existence and the goodness of human life.[14] Moreover, contraceptives may fail and a child, a new human person and uniquely irreplaceable "word" of the all-holy God may be begotten in this touch. Such a child needs a home where it can take root and grow. When nonmarried persons, therefore, choose to couple genitally they further show that they have no regard for the beauty and dignity of the irreplaceable child who may, through their choice, come into being.

Finally, Christians are mindful that in baptism they have been united to the body of Christ and made temples of the Holy Spirit. They realize, as Paul did (cf. 1 Cor. 6), that when they choose to join their bodies to another in genital coition they unite not only themselves but the body of Christ. When Christian spouses choose to give themselves to one another in the marital act, honoring the great goods of marriage, they honor their own bodies and the body of Christ; their "touch" is indeed holy, sacramental. But they realize that should they choose to join their persons to another nonmaritally in genital coition they dishonor not only their own bodies but the body of Christ as well.

The teaching of the Church on sexual morality is too often presented as something negative, a list of "don't's." It is misconceived as something repressive and stifling, hostile to human freedom. Yet in truth this teaching is liberating, life affirming and person affirming. It is rooted in the truth of God's revealing word and in the logic of love, of a love that is not only responsive to the precious worth of the human person but is redemptive and saving. When people take this teaching to heart they discover that it enables them to come into possession of themselves as sexual persons and not let themselves become possessed by sexual urges.[15] They also discover that this teaching enables them to give themselves away to others in love; they learn to love even as they have been and are loved by God in Christ. When they choose to shape their lives according to the liberating truth of the Church's teaching on the irreplaceable worth of the human person and on the beautiful significance of the genital/coital touch, they come to see for themselves why Paul could write to the Romans: "Nothing, neither death nor life, no angel, no prince, nothing that exists, nothing still to come, not any power, or height or depth, nor any created thing, can ever come between us and the love of God made visible in Christ Jesus our Lord" (Romans 8:38-39).

NOTES

[1] As St. Thomas said, "Christus maxime sapiens et amicus est." *Summa Theologiae*, 1-2, q. 108, a. 4.

[2] Pope John Paul II has devoted many of his Wednesday conferences to developing a theology of the body. In these conferences he has stressed that the body is the expression of the human person, a dimension of our personal existence and in no way something other *than* the person or a tool or instrument *of* the person. The first cycle of his talks on this subject has been published under the title *The Original Unity of Man and Woman* (Boston: Daughters of St. Paul, 1981); and the second cyle appeared under the title, *Blessed are the Pure of Heart* (Boston: Daughters of St. Paul, 1983). An excellent synthesizing article of very great help and value is that of Richard Hogan, "A Theology of the Body," *Fidelity* 1.1 (December, 1981), 10-15, 24-27.

[3] Note the significance of *Familiaris Consortio*, n. 11: "Sexuality . . . is by no means something purely biological, but concerns the innermost being of the human person as such."

[4] Among excellent works on the significance and meaning of love are the following: C. S. Lewis, *Four Loves* (New York: Macmillan, 1965); Josef Pieper, *About Love* (Chicago: Franciscan Herald Press, 1976); Robert Johann, *The Meaning of Love* (New York: Paulist, 1968); Karol Wojtyla (Pope John Paul II), *Love and Responsibility* (New York: Farrar, Straus, Giroux, 1981).

[5] Pieper, *About Love*, pp. 4-5.

[6] *Ibid.*, p. 19.

[7] See, for instance, *Love and Responsibility*, pp. 40-47.

[8] On this matter see Johann, *The Meaning of Love*, p. 52.

[9] Here it is worth noting that one of the most distressing features of some development in contemporary Roman Catholic moral theology is the articulation of the notion that one can rightly choose of set purpose to do evil for the sake of good to come. This proportionalistic approach to moral issues makes of St. Paul's teaching in Romans a harmless, toothless moral requirement, for according to the proportionalists all that Paul meant in Romans was that we ought not to do what they consider *moral evil* (as opposed to a 'premoral' evil such as the deliberate destruction of innocent human life) in order to bring about good. These authors likewise put a handy rider on all the requirements of the Decalogue. Thus we ought not to commit adultery, *unless this is necessary to attain some higher, proportionate good*, and so forth. The proportionalist position is manifest in the works of many contemporary dissenting theologians, for instance, Richard McCormick, Timothy O'Connell, Philip Keane, Charles Curran. A handy collection of essays criticizing this development is found in *Principles of Catholic Moral Life* ed. William E. May (Chicago: Franciscan Herald Press, 1981). For a sustained and systematic critique of proportionalism see also Germain G. Grisez, *The Way of Our Lord Jesus Christ*, Vol. 1, *Christian Moral Principles* (Chicago: Franciscan Herald Press, 1984), Ch. 6 and John Finnis, *Fundamentals of Ethics* (Washington: Georgetown University Press, 1983), pp. 80-108.

[10] The constant teaching of the Church has been that the irrevocable act of choice whereby a man and a woman *choose* one another, forswearing all others, as the one with whom and for whom they will to live until death, establishes marriages. See, for instance, *Gaudium et Spes*, n. 48; *Familiaris Consortio*, n. 11.

[11] The German Protestant theologian, Helmut Thielicke, has put this well: "Not uniqueness establishes the marriage; but marriage establishes the uniqueness." See his *The Ethics of Sex* (New York: Harper and Row 1963), p. 109.

[12] Here I am referring to the way in which *Gaudium et Spes* describes conjugal or spousal love.

[13] *Familiaris Consortio*, n. 11: "Sexuality . . . is realized in a truly human way only if it is an integral part of the love by which a man and a woman commit themselves totally to one another until death. The total physical self-giving would be a lie if it were not the sign and fruit of a total personal self-giving, in which the whole person, including the temporal dimension is present: If the person were to withhold something or reverse the possibility of deciding otherwise in the future, by this very fact he or she would not be giving totally. . . . Thus the only 'place' in which this self-giving in its whole truth is made possible is marriage."

[14] To see more clearly why contraception is a choice that repudiates the goodness of our sexuality as life-giving see the following works (all, by the way, written by married lay people): Germain G. Grisez, *Contraception and the Natural Law* (Milwaukee: Bruce, 1964); Mary Rosera Joyce, *Love Responds to Life* (Kenosha: Prow Press, 1969); Elizabeth Anscombe, *Contraception and Chastity* (London: Catholic Truth Society, 1976); John Kippley, *Birth Control and the Marriage Covenant* (Collegeville, Mn: Liturgical Press, 1978; a reprint of a work originally published in 1970 under the title, *Christ, the Covenant and Contraception*). See also my own *Sex, Love and Procreation* (Chicago: Franciscan Herald Press Synthesis Series, 1976), and Chapter 4 of my book, *Sex, Marriage, and Chastity: Reflections of a Catholic Layman, Spouse and Parent* (Chicago: Franciscan Herald Press, 1982). Much of this literature shows, moreover, the dualism of the arguments for contraception. By this I mean the view that the body, and in particular the power that we have to have give life to new human persons, is merely a tool of the "person." It is this dualistic view that is so sharply criticized by Pope John Paul II also, in the works noted in note 2 above.

[15] For a development of this idea, see my *The Nature and Meaning of Chastity* (Chicago: Franciscan Herald Press Synthesis Series, 1976).

3.
Fertility Awareness and Sexuality

Information on natural family planning aids persons who wish to learn about themselves and their sexuality so that they will be able both to exercise their procreative sexuality in a morally responsible way and to deepen and nourish conjugal love. It would be a serious error to consider the art of natural family planning as a mere technological tool that persons can use to enjoy sex without the fear of pregnancy. If natural family planning were to become a regimen for planned barrenhood, or if the knowledge that it provides were to be welcomed simply as a means of facilitating sexual union and of avoiding pregnancy (for both the married and the unmarried), this would be a terrible human tragedy. In what follows I wish to offer some considerations on the significance of fertility awareness that may be supportive of this judgment.

From the time he reaches puberty until death (or, perhaps, until disabled by certain kinds of illnesses) the human male is, whether he knows it or not, fertile. This is not true of the human female, who is fertile for only a short period each month from the time she reaches puberty until menopause. These facts are humanly significant. They show us that there are two different manifestations of the human person, of the being made in the image of God. Although the facts in question are biological in nature, it would be a serious error to consider them as "merely" biological. Our bodies are not tools that "we," who are other than our bodies, use. In short, the human species is differentiated into beings equal in their personhood but different and complementary in their sexuality.

To be fertile means that one has the sexual power of initiating new human life. The Christian sees this power as a God-given gift capacitating the human

31

person to participate in God's creative power to bring new human persons into existence. It is for this reason that we can truthfully speak of human fertility as the procreative dimension of human sexuality. Fertility, moreover, is not to be considered as a curse or a disease; rather it is a blessing, a divine gift. Here, I believe, the words of Shakespeare's King Lear are significantly revealing. The ingratitude of his daughter Goneril so enraged Lear that in the white heat of anger he pronounced on her a terrible curse:

> Hear, nature, hear, dear goddess, hear!
> Suspend thy purpose if thou didst intend
> To make this creature fruitful;
> Into her womb convey sterility;
> Dry up in her the organs of increase,
> And from her derogate body never spring
> A babe to honour her!

There is something quite remarkable about this sexual power of the human person. If a person chooses to exercise it, he or she can do so only with the help of another human person of the opposite sex. The choice to exercise this power of necessity, therefore, establishes a relationship between a male and a female, thereby simultaneously bringing into exercise another sexual power, the power to enter into a union. Thus, human sexuality is, again, both procreative and unitive.

These two sexual powers are meant to go together. In saying this I do not, of course, mean to say that every time a man and a woman unite sexually they ought to generate a new human life. But I do mean to say that the human sexual powers to give love and to give life are inherently or by their very nature bound together. The link between the unitive and the procreative dimensions of human sexuality is not a mere accident of evolution; it is a part of God's divine plan and is of crucial human significance.

There is something of paramount human significance, crucial to our existence as a species differentiated into male and female, in the fact that a man and a woman can, in one and the same act, both give themselves to one another so that they become one flesh and enter into an intimate communion, "knowing" one another in a very unique and revelatory way, and at the same time communicate life to a new human person. Their power to give themselves away sexually in an act of love participates in their power to give life, reaching beyond them to generate a new human being, a person like themselves, a new image of the living God. At the same time, their power to give life inwardly participates in their power to communicate love.

The generation of new human life is not like the production of a table or a car, for a human person is not a product inferior to its producers and subordinate in value to them. Rather a human person is a being equal in nature and dignity to all other human persons, including his or her parents. Human persons are, as it were, created "words" uttered by God Himself. They are the created words that His Uncreated Word became. Thus human persons, like the Uncreated Word of the Father, are to be begotten, not made; and they are meant to be begotten, as the Uncreated Word is begotten, in an act of love. In short, the generation of new human life is not to be considered as an act of "reproduction" but as one of procreation.

In addition, the infant human person is one of the most vulnerable and helpless of animals. It needs a home where it can take root and grow and develop its capacities. This means that it needs love, for love alone can provide the soil and nurture in which human persons can flourish. The best way to provide infants with the love they need and to which they have a right is to see to it that they are begotten in acts that by their very nature and inner dynamism are also intended to express a unique, special kind of love between the two persons who give them life. The love in question is marital or conjugal love, and so we can see that it would be inhuman or morally irresponsible for one human person to choose to exercise his fertility with a person with whom he or she is unwilling to share life, love and the nurturing and education of a child.

But can a person rightfully choose to exercise his or her sexual power of giving love (its *unitive* dimension) with a person with whom one would not choose to exercise his or her power of procreation? Can one, in other words, rightfully give himself or herself away in an act of love to a person who is not his or her spouse? I believe not, and there are many reasons for this belief, some of them founded on a consideration of the meaning of the human sexual power to give love. But the one that I would like to pursue here is intimately related to the question of fertility awareness, or of our awareness of the fact that our sexuality is procreative in nature.

As noted earlier, the male human person is continually fertile. He simply cannot choose to exercise his sexual power of communicating love without at the very same time choosing to exercise his sexual power of giving life. He may not intend that the act he chooses be procreative, and indeed he may fervently hope that it will not be, but no matter what his intent or hopes his choice to exercise his sexual power of communicating love of necessity brings into exercise his sexual power of giving life. Thus the act that he chooses to do will be procreative at least potentially and hence *unjust* both to the woman and to the child who might be conceived *unless* he and she are willing to accept this new life, or *unless* he knows that she is infertile or *unless* either he or she chooses to sterilize the act of sexual union by contraceptive means.

I believe that it would be seriously wrong for either the male or the female to choose to sterilize their act of sexual union by contraceptive means. To explain fully would take us too far afield here, but, briefly, I believe that it would be wrong because it would in essence mean that they regarded their fertility, their sexual power of procreation, not as a blessing, but as a curse. They would be repudiating a dimension of their being and would, in fact, be refusing to share this dimension of their personal being with one another. And this, I submit, would be making their act of giving themselves to one another in sexual union a lie.

This leaves us with the choice to unite sexually when it is known that the woman is not fertile and to abstain from coition when it is known that she is fertile. If *married* couples choose to do this in order to avoid a pregnancy when there are good and serious reasons for doing so, there is nothing intrinsically immoral. Such married couples are not actively pursuing the good of procreation, and they are acting *non*-procreatively, but they by no means are necessarily choosing to act *anti*-procreatively or *contra*-ceptively. As we shall see more fully in the next chapter, they abstain from coition when it would be irresponsible for them to engender new human life, and they abstain precisely because they do not wish to reject their fertility by setting it aside through *contra*-ceptive, *anti*-procreative acts. They honor their fertility and accept it as a God-given gift enabling them to cooperate with Him in the generation of human life. When they do choose to unite non-procreatively at times when the wife is known to be infertile, they choose to do so in order to participate in the person-uniting dimension of their sexuality. Moreover, should a pregnancy occur, they are willing and able to give the life conceived the home it needs, for they have already made themselves to be a procreative community through their marriage, in which they give themselves, including their fertility, to one another.

But if *non-married* persons were to use fertility awareness so that they can unite sexually without the fear of having a child, they would be abusing this knowledge. Because they are unmarried they have not formed between themselves a procreative community; they have not given themselves to one another, and they are thereby not capable of sharing their fertility responsibly or honoring the procreative good of sexuality. Even if a married couple were to use fertility awareness simply as a way to avoid pregnancies, regarding the time when they must forego the marital embrace as a drudge or burden, viewing pregnancy as a disease to be avoided, they would also not be accepting their fertility as a great gift from God and would be abusing and debasing fertility awareness.

Fertility awareness—our realization that we possess the awesome sexual power to give life—ought to lead to an appreciation and a love for that power, for the God by whom it is given, and for the new human person to whom life can be given by its exercise. Fertility awareness, in short, ought to be pro-procreative, not anti-procreative, and it ought to give us a deeper insight into the beauty and truth disclosed in the fact that our sexuality is integrally and inherently both unitive or love-giving and procreative or life giving.

Finally, fertility awareness reminds us of the differences between male and female. Both are equal in dignity by reason of their humanity and personhood; both are equally "words" of the living God, created in His image. But each is different by reason of their sexuality. Fertility awareness, as a way of *being procreative responsibly*, requires both the male and the female to think about the other and his or her needs. It demands that they know one another, be patient with one another, be respectful of one another. It can thus foster love between them and love for the children they can bring into being by the intelligent exercise of their fertility. Fertility awareness, therefore, can be a means of fostering that love which is properly called spousal or conjugal. It can enable husband and wife to realize that their love is meant to be for life, that it is to grow and deepen, and that sexual marital union is but one way to accomplish this within the multi-faceted covenant of marriage.

NOTES

[1] See Chapter 4 of my *Sex, Marriage, and Chastity: Reflections of a Catholic Layman, Spouse, and Parent*, Chicago: Franciscan Herald Press, 1981.

4.
Conjugal Love

In Chapters One and Two I briefly described conjugal or spousal love. Since the concept of conjugal love is so central to the teaching of the Church on marriage and married life, as reflected in the documents of Vatican II, Pope Paul VI's *Humanae Vitae*, and the writings of Pope John Paul II,[1] it is very important to understand as deeply as we can the reality of this love. My purpose here is to make some claims about conjugal or spousal love and, in terms of this love, about marriage and the meaning of our lives as sexual persons. These claims are the following:

1. Conjugal love can actually exist only between persons who are married.

2. The act bringing marriage into being, is, therefore, not itself properly an act of conjugal love itself but is rather the indispensable prerequisite for the existence both of marriage and of conjugal love and is an act promising this love.

3. Marriage itself is an inherently indissoluble union between one man and one woman, giving to them a new identity and obliging them to love each other conjugally until death.

4. Although married persons are under an obligation to give to one another conjugal love, their marriage does not cease to be should they, unfortunately, cease to love one another conjugally.

5. The conjugal love made possible and obligatory by marriage is an utterly unique form of friendship love, one that is by nature exclusive. Its exclusive character is reflected in the marital act.

6. The human act that is, of its own inherent dynamism, integrally a communion in being and life-giving, is by its very nature the *marital* act.

To attempt to engage in this act non-maritally or extra-maritally is, therefore, inherently wicked.

7. Marriage is consummated by one true act of marital union; sexual union between married persons that violates either the communion-in-being (unitive) or life-giving (procreative) meaning of this act is therefore *not* the marital act and thus violates marriage rather than consummates it.

8. Conjugal love is ordered ultimately to the sanctification of the spouses and, through them, of their families and of the societies in which they live.

1. Conjugal Love Can Actually Exist Only Between Married Persons

In Chapter One, in speaking of Dietrich von Hildebrand's analysis of spousal love, I noted that this sort of love can arise as an *aspiration* or desire in unmarried persons, who desire to give themselves to one another and to unite their lives intimately and fully. Yet as an *actuality* conjugal love is possible only for married persons. There is a true sort of *pre*-marital love between a man and a woman who aspire to marriage and to conjugal love, but this love—which must in turn be sharply distinguished from a mere romantic, erotic attachment—remains *pre*-marital and *non*-marital until the uniqueness and exclusiveness that this love foreshadows and toward which it tends is realized in the act that brings marriage into being, the act of marital consent.[2]

The reason why conjugal or spousal or marital love can exist in actuality and not simply in desire only between married persons is that this love is utterly exclusive in character. As Pope John Paul II has said, "the concept of betrothed [or spousal] love implies the giving of the individual person to another *chosen* person,"[3] one with whom and for whom one wills, forswearing all others, to share one's whole life. And what establishes the uniqueness and exclusiveness of the other, or the spousally beloved, is the act of choice or *electio* that brings marriage into existence.[4] Until this act of exclusive choice is made, persons aspiring to spousal love are not as yet fully established in their uniqueness for each other; although there may be some serious moral obligations between such persons, they are not as yet free to love each other as spouses are. If the deep love that they bear for one another is incapable, because of factors or conditions beyond their control, of actualizing the conjugal love to which they aspire and of which their present love is preamble and foreshadowing, there is present an element of pathos and of tragedy and a need for them to bring an end to their pre- (and hence non)-conjugal love.[5]

2. The Act Bringing Marriage Into Being

Thus the Church has constantly affirmed throughout the centuries that the human reality of marriage is brought into being by the irrevocable act of personal consent whereby a man and woman surrender themselves to each other as spouses, and that nothing whatsoever can substitute for this act of consent, or commitment.[6] This act is unique in that it is the conjoint act of two persons, male and female, whereby they freely give and freely receive the person of the other as a spouse. Through and in it they establish the uniqueness of each other for each other.

Pope John Paul II has emphasized that this act of free consent is an act of choice in his commentary on Genesis 2, which is the story of the creation not only of Man but of marriage. In Genesis 2 we read that Adam, on seeing the being equal to himself that the Lord Yahweh had fashioned for him, exclaimed: "Here at last is bone of my bone and flesh of my flesh. . . . For this reason a man shall leave father and mother and cleave to his wife, and the two shall become one flesh" (Gen 2.23-24). In his eloquent commentary on this passage, Pope John Paul II observed:

> The very formulation of Gn 2.24 indicates not only that human beings, created as man and woman, were created for unity, but also that precisely *this unity, through which they become "one flesh" has right from the beginning a character of union derived from choice*. We read, in fact, "a man leaves his father and mother and cleaves to his wife." If the man belongs "by nature" to his father and mother by virtue of procreation, he, on the other hand, "cleaves" by *choice* to his wife (and she to her husband).[7]

Through this act of choice, an act akin to the act whereby God has irrevocably chosen us to be His people and the spouse of His only-begotten Son, the man and the woman give to themselves a new identity: the man becomes *this* woman's *husband*, she becomes *this* man's *wife*, and together they become *spouses, coniuges*. Since this is an act of irrevocable personal consent, through it the man and the woman give to one another their own "word" or person.[8] In and through this act of choice they promise conjugal or marital love to one another, and by virtue of this act and of the marriage that it brings into being they have henceforward the obligation and indeed the freedom to love one another with conjugal or marital love.

3. Marriage as an Inherently Indissoluble Union

The reality brought into being by the act of irrevocable personal consent of the man and the woman giving to and receiving from one another their very selves is the covenant of marriage, an "intimate partnership of life and of conjugal love."[9] This human reality can rightly be called covenantal, for in it the man becomes bone of her bone and flesh of her flesh and the woman becomes bone of his bone and flesh of his flesh.[10] As the teaching of the Church makes clear, it is to this kind of human reality and to no other to which the words of Genesis refer (1.27ff, 2.18ff; also Mk 10.6ff and par., and Eph 5.28-33).[11] This kind of human reality is by divine will lasting and gives rise to, or better *is*, a holy, sacred bond.[12] This kind of human reality, and it alone, is by its inherent nature capable of being integrated into God's saving plan and of serving as the vehicle for a sacramental act of Christ's Church.[13] This kind of human reality, and it alone, can image and make efficaciously present in the world the covenant between God and His people, Christ and His Church.[14] And this is precisely the kind of human reality that a man and a woman intend and bring into being when, forswearing all others, they take one another "for better or worse, in health and in sickness, for richer or for poorer, until death do us part."

To grasp more clearly the truth that marriage is an inherently indissoluble union of man and woman, one rooted, as Pope John Paul II emphasized in *Familiaris Consortio*, "in the personal and total self-giving of the couple,"[15] it is useful to reflect briefly on the meaning given by St. Augustine and the entire Catholic tradition to the good of the "sacrament" (*bonum sacramenti*), one of the chief goods of marriage. As is well known, St. Augustine distinguished three cardinal goods of marriage.[16] These are the goods of the *sacramentum*, of *proles* or of offspring begotten lovingly, nurtured humanely, and educated in the love of God, and of *fides* or steadfast fidelity between husband and wife. The good of the sacrament, for Augustine, consists in the indivisible or indissoluble union of husband and wife. This is the good that marriage *is*, and this is the good that the man and woman bring into being by giving themselves to each other in the act of marrying.

It is a good that St. Augustine more precisely termed the *sacramentum vinculum* or holy bond of indivisible unity between the spouses. This is the good that makes the man and the woman to be spouses and enables them to act as spouses and to bring into being, through their subsequent choices and actions, the goods of *proles* and *fides*. This good of the *sacramentum vinculum*—which in turn is rooted in something of even more awesome dignity, the good of the *sacramentum signum* or sacred symbolism of marriage as a foreshadowing of the nuptial union between Christ and His bride, the Church[17]—imposes upon the spouses, Augustine taught, a holy obligation to remain together. Because of this good, the good that marriage *is*, spouses who separate because of adultery or other acts destructive of the *other* goods of marriage are nonetheless obliged not to attempt remarriage.[18]

Medieval theologians, among them Thomas Aquinas, in reflecting on this good of marriage, developed explicitly an idea implicit in the teaching of Augustine and other fathers and rooted in the teaching of Jesus.[19] This idea is that marriage, as a *sacramentum vinculum* or indivisible union of one man and one woman, not only is the basis of a holy and moral obligation imposed upon the spouses to remain spouses but actually consists in their identity as husband and wife. The *sacramentum*, in short, the good that marriage *is*, is simply another way of viewing the reality of marriage itself. This good is grounded in the *being* of the spouses, the being they freely give to themselves and receive from each other in the choice whereby they establish the marriage and themselves as irreplaceable in each other's lives. Thus not only are spouses not permitted to remarry after any separation, they are simply incapable of doing so precisely because of the *sacramentum vinculum*, the good that marriage is, the good that is rooted in their *being*. And this great truth about marriage is clearly set forth in *Familiaris Consortio*.[20]

4. As an Indissoluble Union, Marriage Abides Even When Love "Dies"

Because conjugal love, a love made possible by the marriage itself and a love that spouses are obliged to foster in their lives, is so crucial, some contemporary theologians claim that it belongs to the *essence* of marriage. They then argue that when this love is irretrievably lost[21] or when it dies, the marriage is no longer in being. Thus Bernard Häring writes as follows:

> Is a marriage which is thoroughly destroyed *and dissolved* (emphasis added), and therefore cannot possibly be brought to life still an existing marriage? Is it still a visible sign, a "sacrament" of God's presence among these two people? Is it still an existing marriage in the sense that the Church cannot allow or tolerate a "real" marriage, that is, a marriage that really could be lived? I do not have the answers to these questions, but I think there is some probability in the following opinion. . . . . marriage is dissolved not only by physical death; it is destroyed, more than by physical death, by civil death (such as a lifelong condemnation to jail for a criminal) and by the total moral death of a marriage.[22]

The opinion Häring advances here is, unfortunately, not uncommon among theologians today. One writer, Theodore Mackin, S.J., even argues that his opinion is set forth in the teaching of Vatican II (!), asserting that "since, according to *Gaudium et Spes*, a marriage is to be understood as an intimate community of life and marital love, *it can dissolve and disintegrate* (emphasis added)," for instance when the love between the spouses disappears.[23]

Vatican II's teaching will soon be examined. Yet I think it is important first to note some observations that Joseph Card. Ratzinger has made about this "opinion," because I believe that he has put his finger on the source of these theologians' error. Commenting on Häring's position, Ratzinger rightly noted that his analysis of indissolubility and of marriage is predicated upon an uncritical acceptance of a contemporary sort of philosophy that ignores the deeper dimensions of human life and experience and *limits the real and important simply to whatever may be occupying conscious thinking and living at the present moment.*[24] This superficial understanding of marriage and human existence, it should be noted, is precisely what John Paul II, both as a moral philosopher prior to his election as Pope and as universal teacher of the Church, has been at pains to unmask as inimical to human dignity and freedom.[25]

As far as Vatican Council II's teaching on marriage is concerned, *Gaudium et Spes*, while speaking eloquently on the subject of marital or spousal love, was very clear in affirming, in company with the entire Catholic tradition, that "marriage is an institution confirmed by divine law and *receiving its stability*, even in the eyes of society, *from the human act by which the partners mutually surrender themselves to each other; for the good of partners, of the children, and of society, this sacred bond no longer depends on human decisions alone*" (emphasis added).[26]

The teaching of the Church on this matter, one rooted in a respect for human persons and human freedom and the reality of marriage, runs counter to the superficial philosophy of our day, a philosophy that has, unfortunately, exerted considerable influence on some theologians and canonists. In order to clear confusion and bring to this issue the light of intelligence, Pope Paul VI found it necessary, in addressing the members of the Roman Rota or marriage tribunal, to reject

> without qualification the idea that if a subjective element (conjugal love especially) is lacking in a marriage, the marriage ceases to exist as a juridical reality which originated in a consent once and for all efficacious. No, the juridical reality continues to exist in complete independence of love, it remains even though love may have totally disappeared. *For, when spouses give their free consent, they are entering into and making themselves part of an objective order or "institution" which transcends them and does not in the slightest depend on them*

as far as its nature and special laws are concerned. The institution of marriage does not originate in the free will of men but in God who willed it to have its own laws (emphasis added). Spouses, for the most part, spontaneously and freely acknowledge these laws and praise them; in any event, they must accept them for their own good and that of their children and society. Love ceases to be a purely voluntary affection and becomes a binding duty.[27]

It is, indeed, tragic when married persons do not love one another, when they fail, through *their choices*, to give the love that they have promised, the love they are capable of giving precisely because they are married. Their marriages are, of course, unhappy. Yet even they cannot gainsay the fact that they are married, and they are married precisely because through a free act of choice they "entered into marriage," bringing into being a new human reality, marriage itself, and giving to themselves an identity that they simply cannot, by an act of will, blot out. A spouse can no more become an ex-spouse than a father can become, by an act of his will or anyone else's will, become an ex-father or a mother become an ex-mother.[28] A spouse may be a *bad* spouse, as a father or mother may be a *bad* father or mother, but their being bad does not mean that they are no longer spouses or fathers or mothers. Common sense, as well as the teaching of the Church, makes this clear.

Moreover, precisely because their marriage endures, spouses are capable of giving to one another spousal love. Precisely because marriage has God, not man, as its author, it is a reality open to *His* redemptive and healing love, and the spouses, with *His* help, which He is always prompt to give, can redeem their love and renew their life together.[29]

5. The Uniqueness of Conjugal Love

Conjugal or marital love is unique because it is exclusive. Its exclusive character, however, needs to be understood rightly. Husband and wife are not, through conjugal love, locked in an *égoisme à deux* and through it cut off from friendship with other persons.[30] To the contrary, they are enabled, precisely in virtue of their conjugal love, one "merging the human with the divine" and a far different thing from mere romantic attachment,[31] to realize "the goodness and loveableness of all people, in fact, of all living things."[32] Nor is conjugal love exclusive in the sense that husband and wife are the "property" of each other. Such possessive language is utterly foreign to and destructive of true conjugal love.[33]

Conjugal love is exclusive because of the irrevocable choice that the spouses have already made of one another; it is exclusive both because it is an intimate sharing by the spouses of their whole life in a communion of being and because it is a personal sharing that by its very nature is ordered to giving to and sharing life with new human persons.[34] The reason why conjugal love is exclusive in this sense can best be grasped by reflecting on the meaning of the act that specifies this love by uniquely participating in and expressing it, and to which it dynamically inclines the spouses, namely the marital or conjugal act. Although the spouses may freely choose never to engage in this act,[35] and although this act is not necessarily the *greatest* expression of conjugal love,[36] it is certainly true that conjugal love is inherently inclined toward and specified by this act, whereby it is uniquely expressed and perfected.[37]

The marital act is the act of marital coition. This act exhibits or symbolizes the exclusive character of conjugal love both as a communion in being (conjugal love as unitive) and as a life-giving and life-sharing reality (conjugal love as procreative). This is the meaning rooted in the marital act and discernible in it; it is not a meaning arbitrarily imposed upon or given to the act. The act is unitive, i.e., a *person-uniting* act or an intimate sharing of personal life, because through it and in it the spouses come to "know" each other in a unique way—as Pope John Paul II has luminously observed in his deeply probing analyses of the marital act.[38] In it they disclose or reveal themselves to each other and open themselves to each other. It is a way of touching each other that is uniquely personal and intimate. In this act they become one flesh, that is, humanly and personally one; through it they renew the covenant they have made with each other in the act that made them to be husband and wife.[39]

This act is procreative insofar as through it they "submit to the blessing of fertility,"[40] exercising their power of procreation, a personal sexual power and not a merely reproductive function, a power given to them by God, whose own love is the fountain and origin of conjugal love,[41] and who has given them the marvelous personal and sexual power of procreation precisely so that He might share with them His own creative love.[42]

The marital act is, therefore, integrally unitive and procreative[43] and exhibits the exclusive nature of conjugal love insofar as spouses alone are capable of loving each other and obliged to love each other exclusively, and insofar as spouses alone are capable of giving to each other procreative love, that is, a love capable of giving life to new human persons and of sharing life and love with those persons. Spouses alone are capable of this because marriage, and marriage alone, both establishes the uniqueness of spouses for each other and capacitates them for procreative-parenting acts. Persons who are not married may have sexual intercourse, but their acts do not and cannot express an exclusively unitive love; unmarried persons may also generate life through genital intercourse, but their acts are not acts of procreative love because they are not capable of giving to the life they generate the home it requires to develop the potential it has properly.

6. The Inherent Wickedness of Non-Marital Sexual Intercourse

The exclusive character of conjugal love as exhibited in the marital act provides the reasons why sexual coition that is non-marital is inherently wicked. Non-marital sexual coition desecrates the meaning that human sexual coition is meant to have, and it does so because it violates its unitive (communion-in-being) and procreative (life-giving) meanings. Although there may be some tenderness and affection between non-married persons who choose this act (adultery and fornication differ from rape, after all), there can be no authentic love in it precisely because it is both an offensive personal touch, even if it is not subjectively experienced as such, and threatens the good of any human person who may come into being as a result of this act.

It is an offensive touch because it is a touch between persons who are *not*, precisely because they are not spouses, joined in a covenant of love and personally dedicated to each other. One human person can hardly be said to love another with any depth or understanding (to observe what John Paul II has termed the "personalistic norm"[44]) unless he or she is willing to be with and for that person, ready to sacrifice for him or her when the need arises, ready to forgive and to seek reconciliation if needed, ready to suffer and even to die. Coition, as a deed revelatory of one's personal being and as an exposure of one's own vulnerability, is offensive touching unless the persons choosing it regard each other as *irreplaceable and non-substitutable persons*. When non-married individuals choose to touch each other in this way, they do so not as irreplaceable and non-substitutable persons—for they have not made each other irreplaceable and non-substitutable by an act of irrevocable personal consent—but rather as replaceable and susbstitutable individuals.

To choose to touch coitally if one is non-married is also to violate the good of *proles*, of children, of the procreative meaning of sexual coition. It is to violate this good precisely because the irreplaceable and non-substitutable person who can be begotten in this act will lack the home where it can be nourished humanely and educated in the love of God.

Thus non-marital sexual coition is, as we are told in *Familiaris Consortio*, a "lie," because it is "not the sign and fruit of a total personal self-giving."[45]

7. The Consummation of Marriage by the Marital Act

Today there is some debate going on about the "consummation" of marriage, with some suggesting that marriage is not consummated until it is "psychically" consummated, and presumably this may not be accomplished until many years have gone by.[46] Indeed, on this view, it is quite difficult to determine whether any marriages are truly consummated or not.

This view, favored by those who also like to claim that marriages "dissolve" when love between the spouses ceases or is "irretrievably lost," is in my judgment dangerously subversive and detrimental to the reality both of marriage and marital love. I believe that marriage, the intimate partnership of live and love, is consummated by one act of truly *marital* intercourse, by one marital act. But a *marital* act is an act of sexual union between spouses that participates in the marriage itself and is open to the goods of marriage. It is, thus, an act that reveres the unitive and procreative meanings of coition, of marriage and marital love. An act of coition between spouses that is *anti*-unitive or *anti*-procreative is, therefore, an act that violates the marital covenant itself. Such an act, consequently, may be a sexual act, but it is not a *marital* act, and because it is not marital it does not consummate the marriage.[47] Thus an act of sexual coition imposed upon one of the spouses against his or her reasonable will would violate the unitive meaning of the marital act and would hence not be *marital*.[48] Acts of contraceptive intercourse, insofar as these are *anti*-procreative,[49] also violate the procreative meaning of coition and are, consequently, not marital in nature and fail to consummate the marriage.[50]

8. Conjugal Love and Sanctification

True conjugal love is an "eminently human love," a love that ultimately arises in the love of God Himself,[51] and a love that is enriched and ruled by "the redemptive power of Christ and the salvific action of the Church."[52] It is, therefore, a love that consists "in the mutual interior conformation of husband and wife, the persevering endeavor to bring each other to the state of perfection."[53] It is a love that is ultimately ordered to the deification and sanctification of the spouses, for this is the will of God. This love is a truly sacramental love. It is a love made possible by that human reality—marriage—which by its inherent trust is capable of being caught up into God's covenant of grace and love and which actually has, so the Church insists, been touched by the grace of Christ and made by Him into a sacrament, one that can truly be termed the "sacrament of divine friendship."

In addition, the spouses are called upon not only to sanctify each other but their children. This great truth is richly developed in Part Three of *Familiaris Consortio*,[54] and it is a truth rooted in the Scriptures, in the teaching of St. Paul that spouses and their children can be *made holy* by the love and faith of one of the spouses.[55] Marriage and marital love are, therefore, truly sacramental in characer and inwardly participate in the saving love and grace of God made visible for us in Christ Jesus, indissolubly wedded to us in and through His bride, the Church.

Notes

[1] Vatican Council II, *Gaudium et Spes*, n.. 49, 50; Pope Paul VI, *Humanae Vitae*, n. 9; Pope John Paul II, *Familiaris Consortio*, nn. 18-21.

[2] The subject of pre-marital love as preparing for marriage has not, unfortunately, been the subject of much recent discussion. An interesting and thoughful presentation is provided, however, in the S.T.D. dissertation of Michael F. McAuliffe, *Catholic Moral Teaching on the Nature and Object of Conjugal Love* (Studies in Sacred Theology, Series 3, no. 79; Washington, D.C.: The Catholic University of America Press, 1954), pp. 1-27.

[3] Karol Wojtyla (Pope John Paul II), *Love and Responsiblity* (New York: Farrar, Straus, Giroux, 1981), p. 98.

[4] As the German Protestant theologian, Helmut Thielicke, put it: "not uniquiness establishes the marraige, but marriage establishes the uniqueness." In his *The Ethics of Sex* (New York: Harper and Row, 1963; reprint Grand Rapids: Baker House, 1976), p. 95.

[5] On this it is worth consulting the observations of A. A. Terruwe, *The Abode of Love* (St. Meinrad: Abbey Press, 1970), pp. 39-60.

[6] *Gaudium et Spes*, n. 48, clearly teaches that the intimate communion of life and conjugal love is established by the "irrevocable personal consent" of the spouses. The Church has constantly taught this. A good history of this constant tradition is provided by Edward Schillebeeckx, *Marriage: Human Reality and Saving Mystery* (New York: Sheed and Ward, 1965), pp. 292-347 and by G. Joyce, *Christian Marriage: An Historical and Theological Study* (New York: Sheed and Ward, 1948), pp. 39-84. The Council of Florence affirmed that "the efficient cause of marriage is the mutual consent duly expressed in words relating to the present" (*Enchiridion Symbolorum*, 34th ed., Henricus Denzinger and Adolphus Schönmetzer, Barcelona/Roma: Herder, 1967, n. 1327; hereafter abbreviated D.S.). In his encyclical *Casti Connubii* of 1930 Pope Pius XI stated: "each marriage . . . arises solely out of the free consent of the two partners; and this free act . . . is so necessary for the constitution of marriage that it cannot be supplied by any human power."

[7] Pope John Paul II, Address of November 21, 1979, "Marriage Is One and Indissoluble in the First Chapters of Genesis," in his *The Original Unity of Man*

and Woman: Catechesis on the Book of Genesis (Boston: St. Paul Editions, 1981), pp. 81-82.

[8] On the significance of "word," see John L. McKenzie, "The Biblical Meaning of Word," in his *Myths and Realities* (Milwaukee: Bruce Publishing Company, 1963).

[9] *Gaudium et Spes*, n. 48; *Familiaris Consortio*, n. 11.

[10] On this see Walter Brueggemann, "Of the Same Flesh and Bone (Gn 2, 23a)," *Catholic Biblical Quarterly* 32 (1972) 532-542.

[11] This point is well developed by Schillebeeckx in Volume 1 of his *Marriage* and also by Pierre Grelot in his *Man and Wife in Scripture* (New York: Herder and Herder, 1965). It is strikingly developed by Pope Innocent III in his letter, "Gaudeamus in Domino" of 1201; text in D.S., n. 778.

[12] *Gaudium et Spes*, n. 48, refers to marriage as a *"sacrum vinculum."*

[13] See *Gaudium et Spes*, n. 48: "Christus Dominus huic multiformi dilectioni, ex divino caritatis fonte exortae et ad exemplar suae cum Ecclesia unionis constitutae, abundanter benedixit. Sicut enim Deus olim foedere dilectionis et fidelitatis populo suo occurrit (Hos 2, Jer 3.6-13, Ez 16 et 23, Is 54), ita nunc hominum Salvator Ecclesiaeque Sponsus (Mt 9.15, Mk 2.19-20, Lk 5.34-35, Jn 3.29, cf. 2 Co 11.2, Eph 5.27, Ap 19.7-8, 21.2 et 9), per sacramentum matrimonii christifidelibus coniugibus obviam venit." See also *Familiaris Consortio*, n. 13.

[14] On this see Schillebeeckx, *Marriage.*

[15] *Familiaris Consortio*, n. 11.

[16] St. Augustine, *De bono conjugali*, 32 (PL 40, 344); *De nuptiis et concupiscentia* I, 2 (PL 44, 420); *De gratia Christi et peccato originali* II, 34, 39 (PL 44, 914).

[17] St. Augustine, *De bono conjugali*, 21 (PL 40, 387-388).

[18] On this see Schillebeeckx, pp. 280-287.

[19] Ibid., pp. 141-143.

[20] *Familiaris Consortio*, nn. 83-84.

[21] This is the terminology of writers like Charles Whalen, S.J. in his article "Divorced Catholic: A Proposal," *America* 131 (1974) 363-364, and Richrad A. McCormick, in his "Notes on Moral Theology," *Theological Studies* 36 (1975) 107.

[22] Bernard Häring, C.Ss.R., "Internal Forum Solutions to Insoluble Marriage Cases," *The Jurist* 30.1 (1970) 22.

[23] Theodore Mackin, *What is Marriage?* (New York: Paulist Press, 1982), p. 315.

[24] Joseph Ratzinger, "Zur Frage nach der Unauflosichkeit der Ehe," in *Ehe and Ehescheidung* heraus. von F. Heinrich and E. Eid (Munich, 1972), pp. 52-54.

[25] On this see Ronald Lawler, O.F.M. Cap., *The Christian Personalism of Pope John Paul II* (Chicago: Franciscan Herald Press, 1982), pp. 51-76.

[26] *Gaudium et Spes*, n. 48.

[27] Pope Paul VI, "Address to the Sacred Roman Rota," February 9, 1976;

text given in Odile Liebard, ed. *Official Catholic Teachings: Love and Sexuality* (Wilmington, N.C., A Consortium Book from McGrath Publications, 1978), n. 1608, pp. 454-455. Mackin, *What is Marriage?* makes much (pp. 320-322) of the fact that in this talk Pope Paul VI speaks of the "juridical reality" of marriage, as if this were in some way different from its "human" reality. I believe that the Pope's use of this term is understandable when we realize that he was speaking to a group of canon lawyers. As a *human* reality, marriage has various aspects, among them a juridical one, in virtue of the fact that it is something public, not private, and in virtue of the fact that it has juridical effects.

28 On this see the remarkable essay by the Anglican lay theologian, J. R. Lucas, "The *Vinculum Conjugale*: A Moral Reality,' *Theology* 78 (1975) 226-230.

29 Here it is important to note that Catholic theologians, taking John 15.5 ("Without me you can do nothing") as one key text, have always held that with God's help we *can* do what we ought to do. St. Augustine put it eloquently when he said: "God does not command the impossible, but when He commands He warns us to do what can be done and to ask for what cannot and gives you help so that you can" (*De natura et gratia*, c. 43, n. 50).

30 See Josef Pieper, *About Love* (Chicago: Franciscan Herald Press, 1974), pp. 50-52.

31 *Gaudium et Spes*, n. 49.

32 Pieper, *About Love*, p. 51.

33 This is the view of marriage promulgated by such writers as Nena and Robert O'Neill in their *Open Marriage*.

34 *Gaudium et Spes*, nn. 48, 50; *Familiaris Consortio*, n. 14.

35 On this see Robert and Mary Joyce, *New Dynamics of Sexual Love* (Collegeville, Mn: St. John University Press, 1976).

36 I believe it necessary explicitly to state this in order to demystify and deromanticize the marital act. It is indeed, as *Gaudium et Spes*, n. 49, teaches, a unique expression and perfection of conjugal love; nevertheless there may be times, perhaps for prolonged periods or even for the duration of the marriage, when it would be impossible or unreasonable for spouses to engage in this act. Yet they need to deepen and foster their love for one another throughout their marriage. The care given a sick, senile spouse could well be a greater expression of marital love.

37 *Gaudium et Spes*, n. 49.

38 Pope John Paul II, Address of March 5, 1980, "Analysis of Knowledge and of Procreation," in *The Original Unity of Man and Woman*, pp. 14 6-152.

39 On this see John Kippley, *Birth Control and the Marriage Covenant* (Collegeville, Mn.: Liturgical Press, 1976), pp. 105-113; Dietrich von Hildebrand, *In Defence of Purity* (Chicago: Franciscan Herald Press, 1968), pp. 54-76; Mary Rosera Joyce, *Love Responds to Life* (Kenosha, Wi.; Prow Press, 1970) pp. 8-26.

40 This is the way Pope John Paul II puts it. See his Address of January 9, 1980, "The Nuptial Meaning of the Body," in *The Original Unity of Man and Woman*, pp. 106-112.

CONJUGAL LOVE 49

[41] *Gaudium et Spes*, n. 48.

[42] Ibid., n. 50; *Familiaris Consortio*, n. 18.

[43] On this point it is useful to note what Paul Ramsey observes in his *Fabricated Man* (New Haven: Yale University Press, 1970), pp. 32-33.

[44] Karol Wojtyla (Pope John Paul II), *Love and Responsibility*, pp. 40-44.

[45] *Familiaris Consortio*, n. 11.

[46] This is the view expressed by Mackin, *What is Marriage?* pp. 29-30. See also John Finnegan, "Marriage," in *Pastoral Guide to Canon Law*, a special issue of *Chicago Studies* 15 (1976) 286.

[47] For further development of this matter see my *Sex, Marriage, and Chastity: Reflections of a Catholic Layman, Spouse, and Parent* (Chicago: Franciscan Herald Press, 1981), pp. 86-88.

[48] Here it is important to note what Pope Paul VI had to say in *Humanae Vitae*, n. 13. He wrote: "Indeed it is justly considered that a conjugal act [understood physically as an act done by spouses] imposed upon one's partner without regard for his or her condition and lawful desires *is not a true act of love* (emphasis added) and therefore goes against the requirements which the right moral order calls for in the relationship between husband and wife."

[49] The *anti*-procreative nature of contraceptive intercourse will be developed in Chapters 5 and 6, below.

[50] Since the Church does possess the power, given to it by God, to "dissolve" marriages that have never been consummated, there are important practical implications here.

[51] *Gaudium et Spes*, n. 48.

[52] Ibid.

[53] Pope Pius XI, *Casti Connubii*, D.S., 3707.

[54] *Famliaris Consortio*, n.. 49-64. For an extensive development of this teaching see my essay, "The Role of the Christian Family, Articles 49-58," in *Pope John Paul II and the Family*, ed. Michael Wrenn (Chicago: Franciscan Herald Press, 1983), pp. 167-192.

[55] Here the pertinent Pauline passage is that of 1 Cor 7.4. In his *Marriage*, pp. 161-167, Schillebeeckx offers some excellent reflections on the significance of this passage.

5.
Contraception, Abstinence, and Responsible Parenthood

We live in a culture in which contraception is widely accepted, even by many Roman Catholics, as a perfectly natural and intelligent way of coping with serious difficulties. The attitude expressed in 1969 by Robert Hoyt, then managing editor of the *National Catholic Reporter*, is surely one that is shared by many: "contraception doesn't seem to hurt anyone and it helps solve some serious problems; what could be wrong with it?"[1] In addition, many people claim that there is no moral difference between contraception and periodic abstinence as a means of regulating conception. This view is particularly common among Roman Catholic theologians who oppose the Church's teaching on the immorality of contraception.[2] These people regard periodic continence, sometimes referred to as "rhythm" or "Vatican roulette," as an especially "unnatural" and "insensitive" way of meeting the difficulties married persons encounter in their struggle to exercise parenthood responsibly. One theologian, James Burtchaell, C.S.C., of the University of Notre Dame, voices this view in this way: "Of all these methods of contraception I should be tempted to think of rhythm as the most unnatural of all, since it inhibits not only conception, but the expression of affection. It is . . . a base theology that would want intercourse to harmonize with the involuntary endocrine rhythm of ovulation and menstruation, while forsaking the greater spiritual and emotioanl ebbs and flows which should also govern sexual union."[3]

Many Roman Catholic writers, furthermore, including such well-known and influential individuals as Bernard Häring[4] and Louis Janssens,[5] argue that contraception is morally justifiable when there is a real need to avoid conception precisely because "rhythm" or periodic continence is morally acceptable. They hold that periodic continence is simply one form or method of contraception; it is "natural" contraception as opposed to "artificial" contraception. Since the magisterium of the Church has already approved periodic continence or "natural" contraception as a way of regulating births, they continue, it is illogical to exclude other forms of contraception such as the pill, the use of condoms and diaphragms and spermicidal jellies. In their opinion the choice of a method of contraception ought to be left to the married couple involved.[6] There is little doubt that that the views described here are widely held by many in our culture and by many Roman Catholics.

It is therefore imperative for anyone who wishes to live by the truths taught by the Church throughout its history and reaffirmed in our day by Pope Paul VI in *Humanae vitae* and by Pope John Paul II in many addresses and in his challenging Apostolic Exhortation on the Christian Family, *Familiaris Consortio*, to know why the following propositions are true: (1) there is a crucial moral difference between the choice to contracept and the choice to abstain periodically from conjugal relations in order to regulate conception; (2) contraceptive intercourse is inherently wicked; and (3) the choice to avoid pregnancies by freely choosing to abstain from relations during fertile periods while freely choosing to express marital love in the marital act during infertile periods can be a morally right way of fulfilling spousal and parental responsibilities.

These three propositions are obviously interrelated; and the purpose of this chapter is to show why they are true. Yet before I attempt to do this, it is advisable to make some preliminary observations that will help the reader to distinguish the substantive question at issue between those who defend and those who reject contraceptive intercourse.

Preliminary Clarifications

The debate is *not* over the need to regulate the conception and birth of children. Parties to both sides of the debate recognize that there can be valid, indeed morally obligating reasons, for avoiding a pregnancy. It could be irresponsible for a married couple to allow, through their own free choice, a child to be conceived, not because the conception of a child is an evil—far from it—but because the parents could not, for various reasons, give this child the care and love it needs and to which it has a right, or because the pregnancy might be a serious threat to the life of the mother.

The debate is *not* over the need of married persons to express their love and affection for each other. Husband and wife are obliged to care for each other and to manifest their love for each other. This is particularly true of Christian husbands and wives, for the love meant to exist between them is a love intended to be both a sign and a participation in the love that exists between Christ and His bride, the Church.

The debate *is* over the means or human acts that husband and wife choose in order to be responsive to their call to share their life and love and to communicate this life and love to a new generation of human persons.

1. The Moral Difference Between Contraception and Periodic Abstinence

Those who claim that contraception and periodic abstinence are morally equivalent frequently bring forward two principal considerations. They first allege that the activities are morally the same because the *intentions* of both contracepting couples and of spouses who practice periodic continence in order to regulate conception are the same. They then assert that the two are morally equivalent because they lead to the same result, namely, the avoidance of conception.[7]

The first of these assertions is plausible only because those who make it play on the ambiguity of the term *intention*, thereby confusing the whole matter. The fallacious character of this allegation has been lucidly demonstrated by the brilliant English philsopher Elisabeth Anscombe, who puts the matter this way:

> The reason why people are confused about intention, and why they sometimes think there is no difference between contraceptive intercourse and the use of infertile times to avoid contraception, is this. They don't notice the difference between "intention" when it means the intentionalness of the thing you're doing—that you're doing *this* on purpose—and when it means a *further* or *accompanying* intention *with* which you do the thing. For example, I make a table; that's an intentional action because I am doing just *that* on purpose. I have the *further* intention of, say, earning my living, doing my job *by* making the table. Contraceptive intercourse and intercourse using infertile times may be alike in respect of *further* intention, and these further intentions may be good, justified, excellent. This the Pope (Paul VI in *Humanae Vitae*) has noted. He sketched such a situation and said: "It cannot be denied that in both cases [contracepting couples and spouses using infertile times] the married couple, for acceptable reasons," (for that's how he imagined the case) "are perfectly clear in their intention to avoid children and mean to secure that none will be born."[8]

Anscombe's point is quite clear. The term *intention* can refer either to the intention to do *this* (in this case, either to contracept or to abstain from marital relations during fertile times) or to the *further* intention *with* which one does *this intentional deed*. The *further* intention is one thing (and it can be either good or bad) and the present intention to do this is another (and it can be either good or bad). The contraception advocate seeking to show the moral equivalence of contraception and periodic abstinence fails to distinguish between the two sorts of intentions and claims fallaciously that the *acts chosen* (the intention to contracept and the intention to abstain during fertile times) by contraceptors and by periodic abstainers are the same because the *further* intentions of both may well be, as Pope Paul VI himself acknowledges, the same.

Further clarification of this matter may be possible if we call the *further intentions* of both contracepting couples and those practicing periodice continence their *motives* for acting and call their *present intentions* to do what they do (namely, contracept or abstain at fertile times) the *acts* or *means* they choose to attain their further intentions or motives.

When the motivations for avoiding conception are good, we can then say that contraceptors and periodic abstainers equally *mean* well.[9] But one's motive or one's meaning well is not the only nor indeed the morally decisive consideration in determining the morality of one's acts. Motives and their meaning are one thing, whereas the acts that one chooses to do in order to realize one's motives are another.

It is obviously possible for a well-motivated person to do something that he or she ought not to do. Let me illustrate this by looking at ways in which we may choose to express our compassion and love for a dying person. We may unfortunately choose to kill him "mercifully" in order to relieve him of the suffering he may be experiencing. If we do so, our act may indeed have been well motivated (our *further* intention may have been good), for we are choosing to kill him not because we dislike him but rather because we want to end his suffering. But the act we choose to do (our present intention) is without question an act of killing, and it is this act that we here and now intend and cannot not intend, and in choosing to do this specific act we are choosing to make ourselves to be killers. We may, of course, in order to express our compassion and mercy for our dying friend, choose to accompany him in his dying, to care for him in his dying. We may even choose to stop using procedures that are no longer obligatory and in this way "permit" or "allow" our friend to die his own death, but we do not choose to kill him or to make ourselves to be killers. In both instances our motives (*further intentions*) may be the same, but the acts we freely choose to do (our *present intentions*) are quite different sorts of acts.

The same is true with respect to contraceptive intercourse and periodic abstinence during fertile times as acts freely chosen in order to be responsive to spousal and parental obligations. At this point I am not interested in analyzing the moral meaning of these acts of choice (this will occupy us in subsequent sections), but simply in showing that there is a real difference between the choice to contracept and the choice to abstain periodically from marital relations as a means of attaining the goal of responsible parenthood (the further intention or motive).

From this it should be quite clear that the first assertion made by those who seek to show the moral equivalence of contraception and periodic abstinence is fallacious and misleading. What of the second assertion, namely, that the two ways of exercising responsible parenthood are morally the same because both have the same results, i.e. the avoidance of pregnancy?

This claim too is fallacious; moreover, it indicates the consequentialistic, ends-justify-the-means mentality of the proponents of contraception. Our acts indeed *get things done*, that is, have results or consequences, but the moral meaning or intelligibility of our acts is not determined by their consequences. For in addition to getting things done, our acts *get things said*, and what they have to say is of paramount moral significance.[10] We can get the same thing done through quite different actions, and while the thing done may be very good the action through which it is done may be very bad. It was, for instance, good to bring an end to the Second World War. Yet the choice to end this war by devastating the cities and populations of Hiroshima and Nagasaki was not a good choice, and the acts of devastating them were not morally good acts.

Human beings, as Eric D'Arcy has noted,[11] have a propensity to redescribe their actions in terms of their intended consequences or results. Thus advocates of contraception, in particular Roman Catholic theologians who dissent from the teaching of the Church, like to *redescribe*, as Richard A. McCormick, S.J., does, the act, of contraception as a "marriage-saving or stabilizing act."[12] Now, while it may, at times, be quite truthful to describe an act in terms of its results (for instance, it's quite truthful to say that Macbeth killed Duncan instead of saying that Macbeth stabbed Duncan and as a result Duncan died), it is not always truthful to do this. And when we redescribe an act in such a way that we fail to reveal or even conceal the nature of the activity in question, then we are simply being dishonest. I suggest that the effort to describe the act that contracepting couples choose to do as a "marriage-saving or stabilizing act" is quite disingenuous, for in saying this one conceals from the mind *what it is* that the couple is choosing to do (intention in the first sense).

That there is a real difference between contraceptive intercourse and periodic abstinence is demonstrable. In contraceptive intercourse there is a double-barrelled choice: one chooses (a) to have sexual intercourse, the sort of action known to be "open to the transmission of life" and (b) to make this action to be closed to the transmission of life, i.e., to set aside or destroy its procreative character. Choice (b) is what makes the intercourse contraceptive; it is the choice to do something which, as Pope Paul VI put it, "either in anticipation of the conjugal act, or in its accomplishment, or in the development of its natural consequences, proposes, whether as an end or as a means, to render procreation impossible."[13] This is what the contraceptor chooses to do. This is what the contraceptor's *intention*, in the sense of the *present intention* to do *this*, bears on, no matter what his or her *further intentons* may be.

Spouses who choose to exercise their responsibilities through the practice of periodic continence choose to do quite different deeds; they execute entirely different choices. They choose, first of all, *not* to have conjugal relations when there is some probability that conception will result. They obviously choose to do this not because they regard conjugal relations as wrong. Quite to the contrary, they recognize that the marital act is a great good, worthy of human love and respect, for this act is meant to be the expression of the love they bear for each other. Nor do they choose to refrain from this act because they consider conception as an evil; rather it too is a great good, but it is a great good that one can rightly respect and love only when the life conceived can be properly educated and cared for. They thus choose to forego the good of marital relations here and now because they recognize that it would be irresponsible to cause a pregnancy at this time. They likewise choose to forego marital relations here and now because they are *unwilling* to choose to engage in the marital act, the act "open to the transmission of human life," and to make it closed to this good. They are unwilling, in other words, to contracept, to act in an *anti*-procreative way. They refuse to regard their fertility as a disease or curse that they must get rid of.

From the above it should be evident that different sorts of *intentions* are manifested in acts of contraceptive intercourse and in periodic abstinence. Contracepting couples and spouses who seek to regulate conception through periodic abstinence execute different sorts of choices. The difference between their ways of acting are *not*, as Charles E. Curran and others endlessly assert,[14] rooted in the "physical structure' of the acts chosen but rather in the human intentions and choices that are executed. Why the one sort of intention and choice (the contraceptive choice) is morally wicked and why the other (the choice to abstain periodically) is not will occupy us in later sections of this chapter. But I believe that it should now be clear why the allegation of advocates of contraception that the two sorts of acts are moral ly equivalent is fallacious.

Yet before turning to an examination of the morally evil character of contraceptive intercourse, I think it worthwhile to dispose of another argument employed by some, for instance, Louis Janssens and Michael Novak,[15] to equate periodic abstinence with contraception.

This argument alleges that spouses employing periodic abstinence are placing a *temporal* barrier between sperm and egg, in contradistinction to those who place *spatial* barriers between sperm and ovum by use of condoms and diaphragms or *chemical* barriers by use of pills and spermicidal jellies. While the kinds of barriers erected may differ, so this argument holds, the actions are morally equivalent insofar as they entail the choice to erect barriers between sperm and ovum.

This argument is utterly fallacious. First of all, it does not take experience seriously, and secondly it ignores the distinction between what is directly willed or intended and what is not directly willed or intended. It does not take experience seriously because it is an entirely inadequate and misleading description of what spouses who regulate conception by abstaining from marital relations are doing. If one were to tell them that *what* they are choosing to do is to place a spatial barrier between sperm and ovum, they would be quite astounded. For *what* they are choosing to do, as we have already seen, is something quite different. They are choosing, for legitimate reasons, to abstain from the marital act during fertile times, and they then choose to engage in this act, to which they surely have a right, during infertile times. They are not executing a choice to erect *any* barriers, temporal, spatial, or chemical.

This argument also fails to recognize the morally significant difference between what is directly willed and intended and what is not. Contraceptive intercourse involving the placing of "spatial" or "chemical" barriers between sperm and ovum—and I think that this is, once again, a *redescription* of the deed chosen in terms of consequences—of necessity includes the choice (intent) that this act of intercourse be closed to the transmission of human life, that it be *anti*- and not merely *non*-procreative. We have already seen this in analyzing the nature of the contraceptive choice. The direct intention of persons who regulate conception by periodic abstinence is precisely the intent *not* to have sexual relations and *not* to contracept; it is precisely the intent *to abstain* from coition rather than make coition *anti*-procreative. Any alleged "temporal" barrier between sperm and ovum is definitely *not* directly willed or intended by them.

In the foregoing pages I have tried to show that there is a real difference in the sorts of human choices executed and acts intended by those who practice contraception and those who practice periodic continence. Theologians who advocate contraception insist, and rightly so, that it is imperative to take seriously the experience of people in assessing the moral character of human acts.[16] Their problem is that they fail to take seriously—or rather caricature—the experience of married couples who seek to express their love and respect for one another and for their personal, sexual power of procreation (which advocates of contraception depersonalize to the level of a "reproductive function."[17]) by refusing, through the choice to contracept, to rid themselves of it and regard it as here and now not a blessing but a curse, not a good but a disease.

2. The Inherent Wickedness of Contraceptive Intercourse

Contraceptive intercourse, as we have seen, of necessity requires the twofold choice (a) to engage in sexual intercourse, an act known to be the sort of kind of act "open," as Pope Paul VI put it, "to the transmission of human life,"[18] and (b) to make this act to be another sort or kind of act, one "closed" to the transmission of human life; and it is choice (b) that makes the act to be *contra*-ceptive, *anti*-procreative. And it is choice (b) that is, as we shall see more clearly as we proceed, morally wicked. Anscombe has put the matter quite succinctly by saying

contraceptive intercourse is faulted, not on account of this *further intention* [to avoid a pregnancy for legitimate reasons], but because of the kind of intentional act you are doing. The action is not left by you as the kind of act by which human life is transmitted, but is purposely [i.e. intentionally] rendered infertile, and so changed to another sort of act altogether.[19]

In this passage Anscombe does not give the reasons why the choice to make the act open to the transmission of human life to be an act opposed to its transmission is an immoral choice. This is a matter that will be made clear below. Yet it is important to recall here a truth that I sought to develop in Chapter 4 ("Conjugal Love"), where I argued that the *marital act* is one open to the goods of marriage, to the goods of marital faith and love and of children and that the choice to repudiate, in this act, any of these marital goods makes the act not to be the *marital act* but rather simply a sexual act between spouses.

I think it important, prior to setting forth the reasons, grounded in human intelligence and central to the teaching of the Church, behind the judgment that contraceptive intercourse is inherently wicked, first to comment on the defective moral reasoning employed by those who defend contraception. In my judgment there are two serious errors that the defenders of contraception make in their analyses, and both errors are integrally associated with their proportionalistic, consequentialistic mode of moral reasoning.[20] These two errors are *extrinsicism* and *dualism*.

In analyzing the principal reasons why many advocates of contraception allege the moral equivalence of this way of acting and periodic continence, we have already noted the consequentialistic characteristics of their reasoning. They confuse the two senses of intention and they seek to *redescribe* the choice to contracept in terms of the *further* intention accompanying the intention to do this, i.e. to contracept. Thus McCormick *redescribes* the act of contraception chosen by married persons as a "marriage-saving or marriage-stabilizing act"[21] (surely something good), and the Sulpician moralist Philip S. Keane would seem to *redescribe* the choice of non-married sexual partners, particularly teenagers, as "preventing-an-irresponsible-pregnancy"[22] (again, surely something good). This move to redescribe actions in terms of hoped-for results is, as we have seen, a typical consequentialist ploy.

It is also, I submit, a form of *extrinsicism* in ethics. Those who argue that a human act is morally good if the act chosen is the one that will realize the greater proportion of good over evil—and this is the key claim of proportionalists/consequentialists[23]—claim that no human acts, described in nonmoral terms, are intrinsically wicked in a *moral* sense.[24] The act is morally good or morally wicked, they assert, on the basis of the *proportionate good* for the sake of which the act is chosen, and this proportionate good is itself the *further* intention (e.g., in contraception, "saving" the marriage or "preventing" an irresponsible pregnancy) accompanying the intention here and now to do *this* (e.g., in contraception, to contracept). The proportionate good, in other words, is *extrinsic* to the act one is presently choosing to do. I submit that the proportionalist/consequentialist, by making the good one hopes to achieve as a result of choosing to do this specific act the morally decisive factor, eviscerates our choices and acts of their intelligibility. He is interested in what our acts *get done* and ignores what they have *to say*.

When I first raised this criticism against the proportionalist/consequentialist mode of moral reasoning, one of its leading proponents, Richard A. McCormick, author of the exceptionally influential "Notes on Moral Theology" that appear annually in the prestigious journal *Theological Studies*, reacted by asserting that "it no longer serves the purpose of constructive moral discourse to argue" in this way.[25] I believe that his response simply fails to answer the criticism. McCormick himself had written, and it was partially on the basis of what he had written (and never subsequently retracted) that the criticism of extrinsicism was raised, that "it is the presence or absence of a proportionate reasons," i.e., of the *further* good to which the present act is ordered, a good *further* intended by the one *now intending* this act, "which determines whether my [present] action" is *morally* good or evil.[26] Thus to claim that the mode of moral reasoning advocated by McCormick and other champions of contraception entails a form of extrinsicism does not, in my opinion, destroy the purposes of constructive moral discourse. It is simply to take the position seriously as it is presented by its advocates. If it is not a form of extrinsicism to redescribe the contraceptive act as a "marriage-saving or stabilizing act" or as a "preventing-an-irresponsible-pregnancy act," then it is not a form of extrinsicism to describe the act of devastating Hiroshima and Nagasaki as a "war-ending act."

The arguments used to justify contraception are, moreover, rooted in a dualistic understanding of the human person. Proportionalists hold that it is necessary to arrange the various goods of the human person into a hierarchy, to "commensurate" them, and, in cases of conflict (such as the conflict experienced by married persons in carrying out their responsibilities) to choose that alternative way of acting that will serve the "higher" good. The consequentialists contend that the unitive good of marital intercourse is "higher' than the procreative good, and that the latter, too, is served by the choice to contracept in the marriage as a whole.[27] The difficulty with this aspect of proportionalistic/consequentialistic reasoning is that it requires us to "commensurate" diverse kinds of human goods. As Germain G. Grisez, John Finnis, and others have noted, it is simply impossible to carry out this commensuration in the way the proportionalists require, simply because the goods in question are incommensurable. To commensurate the good of procreation with the good of friendship, for example, is like trying to compare the length of a rainbow with the number of pages in this book. One could do this only if one could reduce the things to be compared to a common denominator, and there is simply no common denominator to which basic human goods like life or friendship can be reduced.[28]

McCormick, in fact, has now admitted that it is not possible to compare the different goods of human persons. Yet after admitting this, McCormick continues to affirm that nonetheless, "in fear and trembling, we commensurate." In affirming this, however, he really admits that the proportionalism he advocates is in fact incapable of doing the job for which it was designed. It was intended as a moral method for determining, prior to choice, by intelligent judgments, which alternative courses of action are right and wrong.

Yet he now admits, by saying that "we *adopt* a hierarchy," that basic choices or commitments *precede* our judgments. What the consequentialist/proportionalist does, in short, is to state his preferences. And it is here that the dualism of this position, with respect to contraception, is made manifest. For, as I have said, the consequentialist/proportionalist considers the *procreative* dimension of our sexuality to be measurably inferior to its *unitive* dimension. It is now necessary to substantiate this charge.

Contraceptive intercourse, as we have seen, is *contra*-ceptive because it necessarily includes the choice to set aside or destroy the openness of the act of sexual union to the good of transmitting life. The person who chooses to have intercourse contraceptively is saying that it is *not* good that this act is open to life, that it is *not* good that he or she is fertile. Rather the contraceptor is saying that his or her procreative power, his or her fertility is, *here and now*, not something good, but to the contrary a *dis*value or disease or evil. He or she is saying that fertility is *not* a wonderfully good power of the human person, something participating in the goodness of the human person. It may be a useful good, or *bonum utile*, something good *for* something other than itself, a *functional* good that can and indeed ought to be destroyed when it comes into conflict with what is really humanly and personally good, namely the unitive good of human sexuality.

Those who advocate contraception recognize that this is so. The so-called "Majority Report" of the papal commission on the regulation of natality, which sums up practically all the arguments ever given to justify contraception, makes this abundantly clear. For it is evident that the authors of this report consider the procreative power of the human person "merely" a biological good, a *bonum utile*, not a personal good, a *bonum honestum* or *personale*. They regard it as a "subpersonal" or "subhuman" aspect of the human person that *becomes* personally and humanly good *only* when it is assumed into consciousnes and made the object of personal choice.[30] To regard the procreative dimension of our sexuality as of itself merely biological, is, I submit a form of dualism, a dualism that eventually leads to the position that some *living human bodies* are not persons e.g., the unborn child, the comatose dying individual). This dualist is blatant in one prominent Catholic advocate of contraception, Daniel C. Maguire, who claims that contraception

> was also, for a very long time, impeded by the physicalistic ethic that left moral man at the mercy of his biology. He had no choice but to conform to the rhythms of his physical nature and to accept its determinations obediently. Only gradually did technological man discover that he was morally free to intervene and to achieve birth control by

choice.[31]

To put it briefly, those who accept contraception recognize that it requires an anti-procreative choice, the choice to set aside or get rid of or destroy fertility and the openness of the act of coition to the good of transmitting human life. Yet they argue that this choice is morally good *because* the procreative aspect of our sexuality is not, for them, a personal good but rather a merely functional good dependent for its *human, personal* goodness on other aspects of the human person.[32]

It is ironic that the advocates of contraception, whose thought is quite dualistic, accuse Pope Paul VI, in his reaffirmation of the Church's judgment that contraception is intrinsically immoral, of "physicalism." They claim, as evident from the citation from Maguire, that this Church teaching makes "moral man" the puppet or slave of his "biology."[33] The truth is that the advocates of contraception are guilty of physicalism, for they reduce the human body and the human, personal power of giving life to a new person to mere material instruments meant to serve consciously experienced goods, which for them are the "higher" goods of human existence.[34]

The Church and human intelligence both insist that the human body, bodily life, and the procreative dimension of our sexuality are *personal* goods, goods *of* the human person, not goods *for* the human person. Human intelligence insists on this, as Hans Jonas has eloquently stated in his reflections on the views of those who would reduce personhood to cerebral consciousness:

> My identity is the identity of the whole organism, even if the higher functions of personhood are seated in the brain. How else could a man love a woman and not merely her brains? How else could we lose ourselves in the aspect of a face? Be touched by the delicacy of a frame? It's this person's and no one else's. Therefore, the body of the comatose, so long as . . . it still breathes, pulses, and functions otherwise, must still be considered a . . . continuance of the subject that loved and was loved, and as such is still entitled to . . . the sacrosanctity accorded to such a subject by the laws of God and man.[35]

The Church insists on this, for the Church teaches that God's eternal Word took on human flesh, and the Risen Lord, bodily resurrected, is the first fruits of the dead, and that we, made to be His brothers and sisters in baptism, will rise from the dead and be, with Him, risen living bodies.

The personal goodness of the human body and, in particular, of human fertility, is a theme that runs throughout the writings of Pope John Paul II on human existence, sexuality, and marriage.[36] He teaches us, and teaches truly, that our fertility, far from being a mere biological function, is an integral aspect of the "nuptial meaning' of our bodies, the living human bodies that are made in the image and likeness of God and are in truth gifts from our loving Father.[37]

The choice to contracept, therefore, is a morally wrong choice because it is the choice to set aside or destroy something that is really good, namely our own fertility and the openness of the act of sexual union to the great good of transmitting human life.[38] It is just as wrong to set aside this good as it is to set aside the good of friendship in the act of sexual union, a point that Pope Paul VI makes quite effective in his perceptive account of the meaning of marital life and of the marital act.[39]

For Christians, there is yet another reason why spouses ought not to contracept. As Pope John Paul II has noted, the choice on the part of married couples to contracept entails a falsification of the "language" of marital intercourse:

> the innate language that expresses the total reciprocal self-giving of husband and wife is overlaid, through contraception, by an objectively contradictory language, namely, that of *not* giving oneself totally to the other. This leads not only to a positive refusal to be open to life, but also to a falsification of the inner truth of conjugal love, which is called upon to give itself in personal totality.[40]

The marital act, which ought to participate in and renew the marriage itself, is made to be *non*-marital insofar as the spouses hold back something of themselves.

Contraceptive intercourse is, in short, an instrumentalist or pragmatic devaluing of the great human good of fertility and of openness to the goodness of human life in its transmission. It is thus an *anti*-life sort of act, one incompatible with a love for all that is good and with a love for human life itself.

In concluding this section of this chapter I wish to make some observations on the type of thinking reflected in the quote from Robert Hoyt cited at the beginning of the chapter. Hoyt claimed (and in doing so expressed a very widespread view) that "contraception doesn't seem to hurt anyone and it helps solve some serious problems." I believe that the thinking represented by Hoyt is utterly superficial.

People cannot contracept simply by taking thought. In order to contracept they must choose to do something. Some, in choosing to contracept, choose to employ IUD's or pills. It is now clear that IUD's definitely achieve their goal, birth prevention, not by inhibiting conception but by preventing the implantation of human life already conceived with the womb of the mother.[41] They are thus abortifacient in character, and they surely bring harm to the child conceived. In addition, they frequently cause terrible harm to the women in whom they are implanted. The pills currently used in the United States prevent births in a threefold way. First they inhibit ovulation. Yet, since ovulation may occur, they seek to block conception by rendering the mucus of the woman spermicidal. But, since so many sperm are released, the pills are also designed to change the endometrium of the uterus so that human life already conceived cannot be implanted.[42] Thus the pill too may work by causing abortion, and this is something that cannot be ignored. And the pills hurt not only uborn human life but the women who take them. It thus seems to me that a husband has little love for his wife if he requires or permits her to take pills or have IUD's inserted. His love, it seems to me, is focussed more on what he can get from her than on what he can give her.

With respect to condoms and diaphragms, it is strange that persons who are seeking to love each other should employ them. Does one put on gloves when one wishes to touch a beloved? One does not, unless one is afraid that a disease may be communciated. And this is the problem, for it shows that contraceptors regard their fertility as a disease, something that it surely is not.

Since contraceptive practices place burdens on women that they do not place on men, it is not surprising that the practice of divorce has increased along with the practice of contracpetion.[43] And surely people "get hurt" in divorce. The list of ills that follow the choice to contracept could be continued, but enough has been noted here to show the utter superficiality of Hoyt and those who, like him, opine that contraception "doesn't seem to hurt anyone."

3. Regulating Conception by Practicing Periodic Abstinence Can be Morally Good

We have already seen that there is a real difference between contraceptive intercourse and periodic abstinence from intercourse as a means of regulating conception. We have also seen why contraceptive intercourse is intrinsically evil. And we have also seen that it is possible for persons to abuse fertility awareness and to avoid children by misusing periodic continence. But it is now necessary to show that the choice to abstain from the marital act at fertile times can be morally good.

It ought to be evident that there is nothing inherently wrong in the choice either to abstain from the marital act for morally good reasons or to engage in this act during infertile times. Yet it may be helpful to explain why this is so. I take it for granted that it is *morally wrong* for spouses to practice periodic continence for base purposes (here their *further* intentions vitiate their *present* intentions to restrict the marital act to infertile times).

It is surely not wrong to abstain from the marital act for morally good reasons. One good reason to abstain from this act is the recognition that it would not be responsible, here and now, for a pregnancy to take place, and there are various reasons why a pregnancy, which of itself is something good, is not advisable here and now: the financial condition of the family, the health of the mother, etc., etc. Of course, were one to abstain from this act because one considers it something vile or dirty, something to be "used" only for the generation of children or the avoidance of fornication, then the choice to abstain would be immorally motivated. And the same is true, as we have seen, if the choice to abstain is motivated by the desire (the *further* intention, again) to reject the good of children. Yet it is surely the case that many spouses who choose to abstain periodically from the marital act do so not because of these base further intentions or reasons but for morally good purposes.

Nor is there anything morally wrong in the choice of spouses to engage in the marital act during infertile times. The marital act, as the Church teaches and as theologians have recognized since the time of the great medieval thinkers, [44] is good not only because it is open to the transmission of life but also because it is an expression of marital love. In choosing to have marital relations during the infertile times spouses in no way reject or repudiate the procreative good of human sexuality and of marriage. They do not choose to make their act *anti*-procreative; they do not choose to close it to the goodness of human life in its transmission. It is true that they are being *non*-procreative because they are not pursuing the good of procreation here and now, but they are not being *anti*-procreative. They let the marital act *be* marital, open to both love and life, and refuse to make it, by *their choices*, to be *anti*-life.

Here it is important to note, I believe, that whenever a man, who is continuously fertile from puberty until death, and a woman join in coition, there is the possibility that life may be conceived, for the sort of act they choose is the sort of act that is open to the transmission. It is thus possible that spouses who choose to regulate conception by practicing periodic continence may conceive a child. While it is true that natural family planning methods are just as effective in regulating conception as the anti-life contraceptive methods are,[45] there is always the possibility of a method or user "failure." There will be what contraceptionists call "unplanned" or "unwanted" pregnancies, but what in truth should be recognized (and are recognized, by those who practice periodic abstinence in a morally upright way) as "surprise" pregnancies. Even though this possibility may be low, it is still present, and any spouses who use properly their fertility awareness as a way of meeting spousal and parental responsibilities must realize this.

It is, in fact, the case that those who use periodic abstinence in a morally upright way employ it not only for avoiding a pregnancy when there is good reason but also for achieving a pregnancy. Natural family planning (or the use of periodic abstinence) is, after all, *family* planning: it is predicated upon a respect for the goodness of human fertility, on a love for life and the openness of the marital act to the good of human life in its transmission. It is *not* the same as planned *un*parenthood.

From all this it ought to be clear that the choice to regulate conception by periodically abstaining from the great good of marital intercourse for morally good reasons, coupled with the choice to engage in this great good during infertile times, can in no way be inherently or intrinsically wicked. It may be abused and made wicked because of *further* intentions, but for morally upright spouses who respect the nuptial meaning of their bodies and the great good of procreation it can be a rightful way of exercising both spousal and parental responsibilities. The discipline and personal love that it requires, unlike the undisplined and pleasure-loving practice of contraception, will enable spouses to grow in their love for each other and to realize that there is a time to embrace and a time to express love in non-coital ways.

The moral issues at stake in this chapter are of tremendous significance to the human and Christian community. The arguments used to justify contraceptive intercourse are precisely the same sorts of arguments used to justify premarital, extramarital, and homosexual intercourse,[46] something that the more perceptive champions of marital contraception have themselves recognized.[47]

The Catholic Church has consistently held that contraception is inherently wrong, despite enormous pressures to change this teaching. The courage of the magisterium in resisting these pressures, reflected perhaps most nobly by Popes Paul VI and John Paul II, something for which we ought to be grateful, for at stake is the meaning of human sexuality, of marriage, and of the human person. The human person is inescapably and essentially a body person. Our body, with its sexuality and procreative power, is inherently personal, and contraceptive intercourse is an attack on the inherent goodness of the integral human person.

It is true that the need to abstain from the marital act in order to meet spousal and parental responsibilities and in order to avoid the rejection of the procreative good brings with it "problems" for married persons. Yet it is, I believe, better to say that it brings to them a great opportunity to deepen their love for one another and for the God who gave them the great gift of sexuality, who gifted them with the "nuptial meaning" of the body. It challenges them to put first things first and to shape their lives according to the loving requirements of God's reign.

NOTES

¹ Robert Hoyt, in *The Birth Control Debate*, ed. Robert Hoyt (Kansas City: National Catholic Reporter, 1969), p. 11.

² For example, Anthony Kosnik, et al., in their *Human Sexuality: New Directions in American Catholic Thought* (New York: Paulist Press, 1977) classify "abstinence" as a "contraceptive method." See pp. 114, 292-295.

³ James Burtchaell, " 'Human Life' and Human Love," originally published in *Commonweal*, Nov. 15, 1968; reprinted in Paul Jersild and Dale Johnson, eds., *Moral Issues and Christian Response* (New York: Harper & Row, 1971), pp. 139-140.

⁴ See Bernard Häring, *Ethics of Manipulation* (New York: Seabury 1975), pp. 92-96. He explicitly terms "rhythm" a method of contraception.

⁵ Louis Janssens, "Morale conjugale et progestogenes," *Ephemerides Theologicae Lovanienses* 39 (October-December, 1963) 809-824.

⁶ In addition to the authors already noted, see Michael Novak, "Frequent, Even Daily Communion," in Daniel Callahan, ed., *The Catholic Case for Contraception* (New York: Macmillan, 1969), pp. 92-102, especially pp. 94-95.

⁷ See the essays by James Finn, Michael Novak, William Birmingham, Sally Sullivan, and Mary Louise Birmingham in William Birmingham, ed., *What Modern Catholics Think About Birth Control* (New York: Signet, 1964).

⁸ Elisabeth Anscombe, *Contraception and Chastity* (London: Catholic Truth Society, 1977), pp. 17-18.

⁹ On the difference between *meaning well* and *speaking well* through one's choices and actions see James O'Reilly, *The Morality of Contraception* (Chicago: Franciscan Herald Press, 1975), p. 17. O'Reilly's short booklet is an unusually clear and perceptive work.

¹⁰ On the importance of human acts as revelatory of our being see Herbert McCabe, *What is Ethics All About?* (Washington: Corpus Books, 1969), pp. 92-101; also my own *Becoming Human: An Invitation to Christian Ethics* (Chicago: Franciscan Herald Press, 1975), Chapter Four.

¹¹ Eric D'Arcy, *Human Acts: An Essay on their Moral Evaluation* (Oxford: Clarendon Press, 1963), pp. 1-39; also Paul Ramsey, *Deeds and Rules in Christian Ethics* (New York: Scribner's, 1967), pp. 193 ff.

¹² Richard A. McCormick, "Commentary on the Commentaries," in Richard A. McCormick and Paul Ramsey, eds., *Doing Evil to Achieve Good* (Chicago:

Loyola University Press, 1978), p. 241. Here McCormick is actually speaking about contraceptive sterilization, but his description of contraceptive sterilization would seem also to be his description of contraception as such. See, for instance, the way he describes contraception by married persons in his *How Brave a New World? Dilemmas in Bioethics* (New York: Doubleday, 1981), pp. 426-428.

[13] Pope Paul VI, *Humanae vitae*, n. 14.

[14] Charles E. Curran first levelled this charge against the teaching of the Church on contraception in his 1969 essay, "Natural Law and Contemporary Moral Theology" in the work he edited, *Contraception, Authority, and Dissent* (New York: Herder and Herder, 1969), pp. 151-175. He has continued to make the same charge, despite the many significant rebuttals to it by others (e.g., Anscombe), throughout the years. He makes it most recently in his *Moral Theology: The Continuing Journey* (Notre Dame, In.: University of Notre Dame Press, 1982), p. 144.

[15] This is the argument advanced by, among others, Novak in his essay "Frequent, Even Daily Communion."

[16] Häring, for one, stresses the need to take experience seriously in many of his writings. See in particular his essay, "The Inseparability of the Unitive-Procreative Functions of the Marital Act," in Charles Curran, ed. *Contraception: Authority and Dissent,* pp. 176-192. But note the *title* of Häring's essay. Instead of speaking of the unitive and procreative *meanings* or *aspects* of the marital act he calls them *functions*. For Curran's insistence on the need to take experience seriously into account see his essay "Divorce from the Perspective of Moral Theology" in his *Ongoing Revision* (South Bend: Fides, 1975).

[17] This is, for instance, Curran's usual language. See the essays already noted. It is likewise the way Daniel C. Maguire speaks of our power to give life. For this see the citation from Maguire later in this chapter (cf. note 31, below).

[18] Pope Paul VI, *Humanae Vitae*, n. 11.

[19] Anscombe, *Contraception and Chastity*, p. 18.

[20] Recently Catholic moralists who espouse the position that one can willingly choose to do evil to achieve good have sought to liberate themselves from the label "consequentialists." See, for instance, the following essays: Lisa Sowle Cahill, "Teleology, Utilitarianism, and Christian Ethics," *Theological Studies* 42 (1981) 601-629; McCormick, "Notes on Moral Theology," *Theological Studies* 54 (1982) 69-124g, at 82-91 (in responding to criticisms made by John R. Connery, S.J.), and Philip S. Keane, "The Objective Moral Order: Reflections on Recent Research *Theological Studies* 43 (1982) 260-278, especially pp. 267-268, 270. They do not like the label "consequentialist" because it has connotations of utilitarianism, and they do not wish to be regarded as utilitarians. There are surely differences between the Catholic proponents of "proportionalism" and utilitarians. The Catholic advocates of this way of making moral judgments do not consider consequences the *sole* factor in determining the morality of human acts, as utilitarians do, nor do they accept the hedonistic calculus of

classical utilitarianism. Yet they definitely hold that "proportionate reason" is the "decisive criterion" of the *moral* goodness or evilness of our actions (see Keane, p. 268), and this proportionate reason is identified with the good for whose sake one wills *this evil*. That is, it is identified with the good that one has as one's *further intention* in choosing to *this* deed that one *presently intends*.

[21] See note 12, above.

[22] Keane, *Sexual Morality: A Catholic Perspective* (New York: Paulist Press, 1977).

[23] I take this as a fair way of summarizing the description of "proportionate reason" given by McCormick in his *Ambiguity in Moral Choice* (Milwaukee: Marquette University Theology Department, 1973); reprinted as the first chapter of *Doing Evil to Achieve Good* (see pp. 45-50 in the latter volume). Keane, "The Objective Moral Order" (p. 274, note 42, holds that this is an accurate presentation of the basic idea of proportionalism.

[24] Recently McCormick (e.g., in his essay, "Commentary on the Commentaries" in *Doing Evil to Achieve Good*) and Keane ("The Objective Moral Order," p. 269) speak of intrinsically disproportionate acts and intrinsically evil acts respectively. What they mean is that if the description of the act includes as a built-in goal one that makes the choice to do the evil disproportionate, then the act in question is intrinsically disproportionate or inherently evil. For instance, they would agree that it is *always* wrong to choose *to kill an innocent human person in order to placate a terrorist* or *to kill an unborn child in order to be free to travel to Spain*. They would grant that such choices/actions can *never* be justified. Yet they deny that the proposition, *it is always immoral to kill an innocent human person*, is universally true. It is almost always true, they would grant, but for them it would be morally good to do if by doing so one could realize a proportionately higher good. They would similarly grant that it is always immoral to contracept in order to be free of the burden of a child, but they would not grant that it is always immoral to contracept. It all depends. If contracepting, in their assessment of proportionality, would be "marriage-saving or stabilizing," then it would be morally good. In short, all they are now admitting is that actions described in *moral terms* or in terms that embody some moral assessments may well be regarded as intrinsically wicked or disproportionate. This in no way changes their stance that actions described in non-moral terms cannot be so characterized. Cahill ("Teleology, Utilitariansim, and Christian," p. 615) even suggests that "innocent," may be a "value" term. I do not believe that it is.

[25] I first raised this objection in an earlier version of this essay, which appeared in *Faith and Reason* 3 (1977). I developed it in my "Modern Catholic Ethics: The New Situationism," *Faith and Reason* 4.2 (1978) 21-38 and again in "The Moral Meaning of Human Acts," *Homiletic and Pastoral Review* 79 (October, 1979) 310-327. McCormick offered his rejoinder, cited in the text, in his "Notes on Moral Theology," *Theological Studies* 39 (1978) 101-102.

[26] McCormick "Ambiguity in Moral Choice," in *Doing Evil to Achieve Good*,

p. 29 (it is on p. 53 of *Ambiguity in Moral Choice* as published by Marquette University Theology Department).

[27] This is substantively the argument set forth in the paper popularly known as the "Majority Report" of the papal commission on natality. It is most clearly developed in the paper entitled "The Question Is Not Closed" and found in Hoyt, ed., *The Birth Control Debate.*

[28] Germain G. Grisez, "Against Consequentialism" *American Journal of Jurisprudence* 23 (1978) 21-72; Grisez, with Joseph M. Boyle, in their *Life and Death With Liberty and Justice: A Contribution to the Euthanasia Debate* (Notre Dame, In.: University of Notre Dame Press, 1978) pp. 346-354; John Finnis, *Natural Law and Natural Rights* (Oxford: Clarendon Law Series; Oxford University Press, 1980), pp. 111-118.

[29] McCormick "Commentary on the Commentaries," in *Doing Evil to Achieve Good*, p. 227.

[30] See the "Majority Report," "The Question is Not Closed," in *The Birth Control Debate*, pp. 70-71. The "Report" verbally affirms the unity of the person at the *beginning* of paragraph 3 (p. 70 of Hoyt), but succeeds in contradicting this affirmation in the course of paragraphs 3 and 4. For a more detailed critique of this "Report" see my *Sex, Love and Procreation* (Chicago: Franciscan Herald Press, 1976).

[31] Daniel C. Maguire, "The Freedom to Die," in *New Theology Number 10*, ed. by Martin Marty and Dean Peerman (New York: Macmillan, 1973), p. 188 (Maguire's essay originally appeared in the August 11, 1972 issue of *Commonweal*).

[32] Here it is worth noting the very perceptive (and prophetic) observations concerning "situationism" made by Germain G. Grisez in his *Contraception and the Natural Law* (Milwaukee: Bruce Publishing Company, 1964), pp. 53-60.

[33] In addition to Curran (see notes 14 and 17) and Maguire (note 21), see Mary Perkins Ryan and John Julian Ryan, "Have You Thought It Out All the Way?" in Daniel Callahan, ed. *The Catholic Case for Contraception*, pp. 103-127, especially pp. 107-110. They contend that the Church's teaching on contraception is based on a Stoic contempt for material reality. They are egregiously wrong!

[34] Here it may be useful to consult my observations about a separatist understanding of human sexuality in my *Sex, Marriage, and Chastity: Reflections of a Catholic Layman, Spouse, and Parent* (Chicago: Franciscan Herald Press, 1981,) Chapter One.

[35] Hans Jonas, "Against the Stream," in his *Philosophical Essays* (Englewood-Cliffs, N.J.:Prentice-Hall, 1974), p. 139.

[36] On this see the marvelous article by Rev. Richard M. Hogan, "Theology of the Body," *Fidelity* 1.1 (December, 1981) 10-15, 24-27, in which he presents a marvelous synthesis of the teaching of Pope John Paul II in his Wedensday Addresses.

[37] John Paul II, Address of January 9, 1980, "Nuptial Meaning of the Body,"

in *The Original Unity of Man and Woman* (Boston: St. Paul Editions, 1981) pp. 106-112.

[38] It is wrong to set this good aside, as it is to set any true goods of the human person aside. As St. Paul teaches, we are not to do evil so that good may come about (Rom 3.8).

[39] Pope Paul VI, *Humanae Vitae*, n. 13.

[40] *Familiaris Consortio*, n. 32.

[41] See Thomas Hilgers, M.D. "An Evaluation of Intrauterine Devices," *International Review of Natural Family Planning* 2 (1978) 68-85 and "The Intrauterine Device: Contraceptive or Abortifacient?" *Marriage and Family Newsletter* 5 (Jan,-March, 1974) 3-24.

[42] See Virginia Gagern, *The Pill and the IUD: Contraceptive or Abortifacient?* (Collegeville, Mn.: Human Life Center Pamphlet, 1978).

[43] See K. D. Whitehead, "The 'Responsibility' Connection: Divorce, Contraception, Abortion, Euthanasia," in his *Agenda for the Sexual Revolution* (Chicago: Franciscan Herald Press, 1981), pp. 101-115.

[44] See St. Thomas Aquinas, *Summa Theologiae*, Tertia Pars, Supplement, q. 49, a. 4. Here I wish to correct an error in the earlier draft of this essay (*Faith and Reason* 3, 1977); there I mistakenly said that Aquinas and other medieval theologians, in company with St. Augusine, required a procreative intent for the marital act to be fully act. It is quite clear that Aquinas and other medieval theologians recognized that the marital act, undertaken either to pursue the good of procreation *or* to pursue the good of *fides* or love, is not only good but holy and meritorious. One could not, of course, be opposed to either of these marital goods. For excellent studies of the the the thought of Aquinas and other medieval theologians see Fabian Parmisano, "Love and Marriage in the Middle Ages," *New Blackfriars* 50 (1969) 599-608, 649-660, and Germain G. Grisez, "Marriage: Reflections Based on St. Thomas Aquinas and Vatican Council II," *The Catholic Mind* 64 (June, 1965) 4-19.

[45] See Hannah Klaus, M.D., "Use Effectiveness and Analysis of Satisfaction Levels with the Billings Ovulation Method: Two Year Pilot Study," *Fertility and Sterility* 28 (1977) 1039.

[46] See the arguments, for example, of Keane in his *Sexual Morality*. He argues that the "ontic evil" of contraception is justified by the greater good (proportionate good) of the marriage as a whole, and similarly that the "ontic evil" of homosexual and premarital activity is justified by the "greater good" of a stable relationship and avoidance of promiscuous kinds of homosexual and premarital activity.

[47] Curran clearly recognizes this in a remark that he makes in his essay on divorce, noted previously in note 16. He observed: "History has clearly shown that those who were afraid that a change in the teaching on contraception would lead to other changes were quite accurate" (pp. 77-78).

6.
Church Teaching and the Immorality of Contraception

Three noteworthy essays on contraception were published between the fall of 1980 and the spring of 1981. The first, by Lawrence Porter, O.P., was explicitly an effort to challenge the contemporary consensus on the permissibility of contraception.[1] Although he did not seek to interpret the teaching of the Church, one can legitimately infer that his article was intended to support this teaching. The other two essays, by John T. Noonan, Jr., and John Wright, S.J.,[2] were explicitly concerned with the teaching of the Church as expressed in Pope Paul VI's encyclical *Humanae Vitae*; in the judgment of their authors these essays supported the teaching by providing correct analyses and applications of it.

In my opinion the essays by Noonan and Wright seriously misinterpret and distort the teaching of the Church on this question and do so primarily because the authors fail to understand what contraception is and why the Church teaches that the choice to contracept is morally wrong. Although Porter's essay, unlike Noonan's and Wright's, does not explain the Church's teaching by explaining it away, it too fails to come to terms with the moral issues at stake. In what follows I hope to provide the reasons supporting my assessment of these essays first by taking each essay separately and then by presenting observations concerned with the proper description of contraception and with the moral reasons why the Church judges contraception to be intrinsically disordered, *morally* evil, and hence an act that a human person ought never freely choose to do.

1. Lawrence Porter's Argument

Porter challenges the contemporary consensus that contraception is morally legitimate by arguing that the practice of "artificial contraception" runs the serious risk of depersonalizing sexual intimacy. Porter, in developing his argument, skillfully utilizes perceptive psychological insights of Rollo May that are artistically illumined by Saul Bellow in his novel, *Herzog*.

Porter admirably succeeds in showing that the choice to use "artificial" contractives *can* result in the dehumanization of sexual intimacy and the trivialization of sex. Still the argument he uses does not show that contraception is necessarily immoral; rather it is an argument that can be used to support rather than challenge the judgment that "artificial" contraception *can be* (although it need not be) a morally good choice. It does so because Porter insists in speaking of the regulation of conception through periodic abstinence as "natural contraception,"[3] and because his argument is consequentialistic in nature, drawing its force from the deleterious consequences on sexual intimacy to which "artificial" contraception can and frequently does lead.

Basically Porter argues that it is wrong to use "artificial" contraceptives because they have a tendency to destroy sexual intimacy, whereas "natural contraception" is morally permissible because it does not have a tendency to cause this (presumably, "natural" contraception would be immoral were its use to result in the destruction of sexual intimacy).

A major difficulty with Porter's argument is that it regards contraception as such as morally neutral. It can be morally good, as "natural" contraception is, if it does not result in destroying sexual intimacy; it can be morally wrong, as "artificial" contraception is, because of the risks it poses to sexual intimacy.

I think that those who justify "artificial" contraception will find Porter's analysis akin to their own. One of the major claims made by many who justify "artificial" contraception is that the Church's opposition to their use is simply the result of a "phsyicalistic" notion of the natural law that sees the physical structure of the sexual act as morally determinative.[4] They argue that since the Church permits "natural" contraception, i.e., the regulation of conception through periodic continence, there is nothing wrong with contraception. They then argue that the Church unreasonably refuses to admit that "artificial" contraception can also be morally legitimate provided that those who choose to use such means do so within the context of a conjugal life responsibly fruitful and so long as they are careful to avoid the dehumanizing effects that *may* result from such means. Those who defend "artificial" contraception are ready to admit that one ought *not* to use artificial means *if* their use would result in the dehumanization of sexual intimacy.[5] It thus seems to me that Porter's "challenge to the consensus on contraception," while provocative and in many ways quite perceptive psychologically, leaves the key moral question of contraception untouched. In particular, his effort is marred by his failure to recognize what contraception is and why it is immoral and by his insistence upon identifying the regulation of conception through periodic abstinence with "natural" contraception. I shall return to these issues in the final part of this paper.

2. John T. Noonan's Presentation

Noonan's essay, which has already been cogently criticized in a detailed analysis by Charles E. Rice,[6] begins with the acknowledgment that the teaching of *Humanae vitae* is a "given of Catholic doctrine" and that our task now is to understand properly and apply this teaching.[7] Noonan then proceeds to give his interpretation of the "doctrine" at the heart of the encyclical and to offer some applications of it.

Humanae vitae, Noonan says, offered "a new and distinctive basis for the doctrine forbidding intervention which deliberately deprived *a naturally fecund marital act of fertility*" (P. 21; emphasis added). Note well how Noonan expresses the "doctrine" set forth in *Humanae vitae*; as Rice has observed, "Noonan is stating the teaching in such a way as to foreshadow his own conclusions."[8] Noonan repeatedly stresses that what the encyclical condemns is the "deliberately willed dissassociation between the conjugal act and the *natural rhythm* of fertility" (P. 35; emphasis added; cf. pp. 30, 32, 33). This is what the encyclical condemns because, Noonan contends, the doctrine of the encyclical is grounded in the "natural rhythm of fecundity and infecundity." It is this natural rhythm that "serves as the basis for the symbolic human significance of conjugal acts in which fecundity accompanies the expression of love" (p. 23). The teaching of the Church "builds on," "is based on," and "rests on" the natural rhythm of fecundity and sterility (pp. 22, 23, 29).

Because this is so, Noonan believes that we must, for the sake of accuracy, speak not of "contraceptive" means but rather of "dissassociative means," not of "contraception" but rather of "disruption of the unity" (p. 30). By this Noonan means that the doctrine of *Humanae vitae* forbids any human intervention (contraception as a "dissassociative means") that would deprive the marital act of its fecundity by "dissassociating" the unitive and procreative significance of the marital act during the fertile phase of the woman. One of his key contentions then[9] is that means used to prevent or impede procreation in the marital act during the non-fertile phase of the woman would be morally legitimate and would in no way be contrary to the "doctrine" of *Humanae vitae* (pp. 29-37). Noonan seeks to support this claim by arguing that in human beings God intends fertility and the conse-

quent union of the symbolic significance of the unitive and procreative meanings of marriage and of human sexuality to be present only four days of
the woman's twenty-eight day cycle. Fertility in the woman at any other
time during the cycle is, Noonan asserts, "unnatural" (p. 33), and consequently may be eliminated by sterilizing or "contraceptive" means, and the
choice to do so is morally right and in accord with the doctrine of the Church
as set forth in *Humane vitae*.

There are serious, indeed insurmountable, difficulties with Noonan's
"interpretation" of *Humanae vitae*. The most obvious is that Noonan is simply wrong in formulating the "doctrine" of the encyclical. Noonan, as we
have seen, insists that what the encyclical condemns is any effort to break
the "natural nexus" between conjugal intercourse and procreation, and by
"natural nexus" he means the bond between the unitive and the procreative
meanings of the marital act during the fertile phase of the woman's period,
a bond meant to exist in Noonan's judgment only for 96 hours during the
woman's twenty-eight day cycle. He likewise insists that the teaching of
the encyclical is based on the "natural rhythms" of fertility and infertility
and that Pope Paul VI is not to be taken literally in affirming that "each
and every marriage act (*quilibet matrimonii usus*) must remain open to the
transmission of life" (*Humanae vitae*, n. 11; cf. Noonan, pp. 33-34).

An examination of the encyclical, however, shows that Pope Paul taught
that what the moral law forbids is not simply, as Noonan claims, any
"deliberately willed dissassociation between the conjugal act and the natural
rhythm of fertility" (p. 35), but rather *"every action* which, either in anticipation of the conjugal act or in its accomplishment or in the development of its natural consequences proposes, whether as an end or as a means,
to render procreation impossible" (*Humanae vitae*, n. 14; emphasis added).

Noonan completely ignores the moral significance of an important
passage in the encyclical where Pope Paul clearly shows that it is immoral
to choose to impede or destroy either the unitive or the procreative meanings of the marital act (*Humanae vitae*, n. 13). The point that the Pope is
making—one to which we shall return in the concluding part of this paper—is
that it is immoral to choose to act against the real goods of human sexuality
and of marriage, i.e., the unitive and procreative goods. Noonan's failure
to consider this morally significant passage is one reason why he
misconceives the "doctrine" of the encyclical and the moral issues involved in contraception.

In addition, the Pope does not claim, as Noonan does, that "the inseparable connection, willed by God and unable to be broken by man on
his own initiative, between the two meanings of the conjugal act: the unitive

meaning and the procreative meaning" (*Humanae vitae* n. 12) is based on the "natural rhythm of fertility and infertility" (Noonan, p. 30). Rather the Pope teaches that these meanings are inseparably connected, indissolubly joined; and he insists that only "by safeguarding both these essential aspects, the unitive and the procreative, does the conjugal act preserve in its fullness the sense of true mutual love and its ordination toward man's most high calling to parenthood" (*Humanae vitae*, n. 12). He teaches (*Humane vitae*, n. 13) that these "essential aspects" are safeguarded by respecting them and that the choice to impede or destroy either is what the moral law forbids.

Since Pope Paul recognizes that "God has wisely disposed natural laws and rhythms of fecundity, which, of themselves, cause a separation in the succession of births" (*Humanae vitae*, n. 11), he evidently does not regard this "separation in the succession of births," caused by the "rhythms of fecundity," to entail the dissolution of the inseparable connection between the unitive and procreative meanings of conjugal intercourse or the "openness" of conjugal acts to the transmission of life. Bertrand de Margerie, S.J., and others have properly explained the intention of the encyclical in speaking of the openness of every conjugal act to the transmission of life, whereas Noonan has misunderstood what this means. De Margerie observes that "every matrimonial act should be *intrinsically* ordered to life, to the transmission of life, even if in actual fact, owing to an accidental and extrisic reason, it must remain barren."[10] A conjugal act that respects the gift of fertility, of procreativity, is one that is intrinsically open to the transmission of life, even if conception, as a physical event, does not take place or cannot take place because of sterility resulting from "natural rhythms" or age or disease. A conjugal act respectful of what Pope John Paul II calls the "nuptial meaning" of the body and of the willing submissiveness of sexed humanity to the gift of fertility[11] is one that is "open" to the transmission of life. There is a significant *moral* difference between a conjugal act that is sterile because of natural rhythms, age, or disease and one that has been deliberately *sterilized* by the free choice of the spouses. Although Noonan recognizes the *physical* difference between a naturally infertile conjugal act and one deliberately made infertile by human choice, he does not recognize the *moral* difference between these acts, a difference made by the sorts of choices involved. As a result he seriously misunderstands what the encyclical means when it speaks of the openness of every true conjugal act to the transmission of life and of the "inseparable connection" willed by God between the unitive and the procreative *meanings* of marriage and human sexuality.

Noonans' essay, far from supporting the teaching of *Humanae vitae* which he acknowledges as "a given of Catholic doctrine," substitutes for this teaching Noonans' own doctrine that the natural moral law requires us to respect the goodness of our sexal procreativity *only* during the 96 hours of the woman's peak fertile phase and permits us to ensure sterility by contraceptive means during the rest of her cycle, when fertility is, in Noonans' judgment, "unnatural." Noonan's position is, in my opinion, one that is definitely physicalistic or biologistic in character, locating the root or basis of the Church's teaching on contraception in the "natural nexus" beween the unitive and procreative meanings of marriage and sexuality during the fertile phase of the woman. Noonan ignores the moral signifiance of choosing to act against the good of procreation; because he does so he, like Porter, fails to understand what contraception really is and why the Church teaches that it is immoral—a point to which we shall return in the conclusion.

3. John Wright's Analysis

At the beginning of his essay Wright raises the following question: "Is there a way to affirm the radical intent and importance of Paul VI's specific teaching and at the same time to recognize an objectively legitimate departure from it in certain concrete circumstances, a departure that does not undermine that teaching and render it trivial?"[12]

Wright answers this question in the affirmative. Yet he can give this answer only by providing an interpretation of the teaching in *Humanae vitae* that is, like Noonan's, not an interpretation but rather the substitution of his own doctrine for that of the encyclical. In the course of his essay he also shows that he does not understand what contraception is and why the Church teaches that a contraceptive choice is immoral.

According to Wright the teaching of Paul VI is "an obligatory ideal, a unique embodiment of values that makes a positive and enduring claim upon conscience" (p. 175). The obligatory ideal in question, Wright makes clear several times in the course of his brief article, is "sexual intercourse open to the possibility of conception" (pp. 176, 177). In other words, for Wright the "radical intent and importance of Paul VI's specific teaching" in *Humanae vitae* is to claim that there is an obligatory ideal for married couples to engage in sexual intercourse that is "open to the possibility of conception." Because this is his understanding of the obligatory ideal at the heart of Paul VI's *specific teaching*, Wright then contends that one departs from this obligatory ideal "whether by choosing infertile periods or by rendering fertile periods unproductive" (p. 177). In making this claim Wright clearly indicates that he believes that the choice to regulate conception by periodic abstinence and the choice to do so by using "artificial contraceptives" are morally equivalent. That is, he indicates that, with Porter and others, there are two kinds of contraception, "natural" and "artificial." He believes that either of these ways of departing from the "obligatory idea" at the heart of Paul's specific teaching can be morally permissible provided there are "proportionate, objective" reasons for departing from the obligatory ideal (p. 177). The obligatory ideal of having intercourse open to the possibility of conception is, Wright argues, the type of obligatory ideal that lays "a claim upon conscience and . . . viewed in abstraction from the total situation," is "capable of realization both intrinsically and extrinsically, but considered concretely with all attendant circumstances *ought not to be achieved*" (p. 176).

From what has already been said in commenting on Noonan's essay it should be apparent that Wright has simply substituted his own ideas for the "specific teaching" of Paul VI. His analysis, in particular, (1) misinterprets the meaning of Paul's teaching that every conjugal act is to be open to the transmission of life, (2) fails to distinguish between affirmative duties and negative prohibitions, and (3) shows that he does not understand what contraception is and why it is judged to be intrinsically disordered by the teaching authority of the Church.

Wright obviously believed that by speaking of the openness of the conjugal act to the transmission of life Pope Paul was claiming that every act of marital intercourse must be capable of leading to conception here and now. We have already seen that this is not the meaning of this affirmation in the encyclical. Wright confuses the physical possibility of conception actually occurring (it cannot when a woman is pregnant, beyond menopause, or infertile as a result of "natural rhythms") with the *moral* significance of respect for the procreative meaning of human sexuality and marriage that Paul teaches, a respect that regards this meaning as something good and not to be attacked.

There is indeed an affirmative obligation on the part of married couples to have children, as Paul and Vatican II teach. After all, as Vatican II so strongly insisted, marriage and married love are by their very nature ordered to the generation and education of children and parents are to regard it as their highest mission to collaborate generously with God in raising up new life (cf. *Gaudium et Spes*, nn. 48, 50). Yet an affirmative duty differs in its obligatory character from a negative injunction. The scholastics used to put this difference by saying that affimrative duties oblige *semper sed non pro semper*, whereas negative injunctions oblige *semper et pro emper*. By this they meant we are always obliged to do the good, but that we cannot be doing good all the time, and that at times the pursuit of a given good (such as the procreation of children) might need to be foregone (although never attacked) if its pursuit should entail deliberate or even indeliberate yet disproportionate destruction of other goods. Thus we ought always to tell the truth, but we are not obligated to speak at all times of our lives (and hence to speak truthfully) and there are times when we may rightfully conceal a truth when its revelation would constitute an unjust attack upon a neighbor. In similar fashion, married couples have a positive obligation to have children (as *Gaudium et spes* insists), yet there can be reasons why they can legitimately choose to refrain from pursuing this good, and *they* are to be the best judges of this. Yet Wright insists that the core teaching of the encyclical is the imposition of a positive affirmative duty to engage in marital intercourse that will positively result in conception, and in doing so totally ignores the long-standing and important moral distinction between affirmative duties, such as the duty to have children, and negative injunctions, such as the injunction, given in the encyclical, to refrain from contraceptive intercourse.

Wright fails to understand what contraception is and why the Church teaches that it is immoral. First of all, he identifies the regulation of conception by periodic abstinence with the choice deliberately to render fertile periods "unproductive" (p. 177). By claiming that the specific teaching of the encyclical is an affirmative obligation to engage in marital intercourse that will actually result in a pregnancy, he shows that he does not realize that its specific teaching included a negative injunction, namely that one ought never to choose to repudiate the goodness of human procreativity—the procreative meaning of human sexuality—just as one ought not ever to choose to repudiate the unitive goodness of sexuality.

The Church has always taught that certain sorts of human chocies, such as the choice to kill innocent human beings, to lie, to devastate entire cities along with their populations, and to repudiate the goodness of human procreativity are *intrinsically* disordered and subject to universal negative prohibitions. By claiming that the teaching of *Humanae vitae* is basically the assertion of an affirmative obligation rather than the firm statement of a negative injunction, Wright has simply begged the question, framing it in such a way that his own "resolution" is assured.

It ought also to be noted that Wright presents his view as a "new" breakthrough, a way of affirming the radical intent of Paul VI's specific teaching and of simultaneously asserting an objectively legitimate departure from it in concrete circumstances. Although Wright's own interpretation of Paul's "specific teaching" is novel, his attempt to divine its "deeper" meaning and, in the light of this "deeper" meaning, to justify objectively departures from it in specific cases is surely not, as readers familiar with the abundant literature on the question will easily recognize.

Finally, Wright claims that the encyclical's teaching is true in abstraction from concrete circumstances. Any reader of *Humanae vitae* will see immediately that Paul VI reaffirmed the Church's teaching on the intrinsic evil of contraception precisely as a norm to be observed by married couples in the concrete exigencies of their daily lives.

Concluding Comments: What Contraception Is and Why It is Immoral

Contraception is not the same as birth control. In addition to contraception there are many other ways of controlling births, some morally good, others morally wicked. One can control births by abortion—a morally evil way—or by abstaining from coition, either permanently or periodically. Neither of these latter methods of birth control is contraceptive.

Contraception does prevent birth, but does so in a specific way. It does so in a way that entails a twofold choice. There is first the choice to have intercourse, something known to be intimately related to the generation of life. There is secondly the choice to impede procreation, whether in anticipation of the act of intercourse, during it, or while it is having its natural consequences, and to do so precisely because one does not want intercourse to lead to the generation of life and one believes that the intercourse one has freely chosen is the kind of act that may do this. It is thus proper to speak of contraceptive intercourse.

What makes the contraceptive act to be *contraceptive* or *anti-procreative* is the choice, freely made, to get rid of, here and now, the procreativity of a freely chosen act of coition. The contraceptive act is not simply nonprocreative (i.e., one that does not in fact result in pregnancy) but *anti-procreative*, i.e., an attack on the goodness of the procreativity of marriage and of human sexuality. It is an act in and through which one says that it is *not* good here and now to be fertile. It is an act in and through which one says that it is *not* good that coition is open to the transmission of life.

It is for this reason that Paul VI and the Church teach firmly that the contraceptive choice is intrinsically disordered. To choose to act in this way is to choose to act against something really good, and good not merely in an instrumental way but personally and humanly good. The procreative meaning of our sexuality and of the marital act is not a good of the biological order, subhuman and subpersonal in character, but is rather a good of the human person, a good participating in the goodness of the human person and of God, the author of our procreativity. The contraceptive choice is a choice to reject this good of the human person, of human sexuality, and of marriage.

Yet, the Church again teaches, we are not to choose to do evil for the sake of good to come. Thus the choice to contracept, as the choice to kill an innocent person, is one that is intrinsically disordered, *morally* evil, one that we ought never freely choose to make if we wish to order our lives according to the objective norms of morality.

This is the teaching of *Humanae vitae*, a teaching that stresses the *moral* wickedness of the contraceptive, anti-procreative choice. This aspect of the Church's teaching is totally ignored in the essays under consideration, and for this reason all fail to come to terms with the moral issue of contraception.

People can definitely misuse natural family planning and immorally refuse to have children by abstaining from marital coition during the fertile period of the woman. Such people may reflect an "anti-baby" mentality that is worse than the contraceptive mentality reflected, willy-nilly, by those who choose to contracept. Some people may also reflect a contraceptive mentality in their misuse of natural family planning insofar as they prefer it to chemical and barrier methods for hygienic or aesthetic reasons or fear that the latter may inhibit sexual intimacy or result in health problems. But these abuses of natural family planning do not prove that the regulation of conception by periodic abstinence is, as Porter and Wright claim, "natural contraception." This claim rests on the assumption that periodic abstinence is contraceptive because the choice to abstain can be used to avoid a pregnancy when there are serious and legitimate reasons to avoid one and on the assumption that every way of avoiding a pregnancy is contraceptive. The reasoning based on these assumptions is fallacious, as can be shown by formulating explicitly the implicit argument. It can be put as follows: All contraceptive acts are ways of avoiding a pregnancy. But all use of periodic abstinence is a way of avoiding a pregnancy. Therefore all use of periodic abstinence is contraceptive. This is like arguing: All eagles are birds. All pigeons are birds. Therefore all pigeons are eagles.[13]

Distinctly different kinds of human choices are entailed in contraceptive intercourse and in the use of periodic abstinence to regulate conception. In contraceptive intercourse, as we have seen, the explicit choice is to destroy the procreative potential of the genital embrace that is also freely chosen; it is this choice that makes the act *contra*-ceptive, *anti*-procreative. Married couples who practice periodic abstinence make different choices. They choose to abstain from the marital act when they have good reasons to believe that this act may result in a pregnancy and they have legitimate reasons for avoiding a pregnancy. They abstain from the act not because they consider it wrong or repugnant—far from it; they abstain because they realize that to express their love for one another in the marital act here and now would be irresponsible (or would require them to contracept and be morally irresponsible in that way). They recognize that conception and pregnancy are great goods, but they realize that pursuing these goods here and now would be irresponsible. They also realize that it would be irresponsible and morally wicked to repudiate the goodness of their procreativity by contracepting. They then choose to express their love for one another in the marital act when they can reasonably believe that conception will not occur in order to participate in legitimate goods of marriage *without setting themselves against the good of their own procreativity or the openness of their expression of marital love to the good of transmitting life*. They do not choose to be *anti*-procreative, *contra*-ceptive. In short, they refuse to contracept, and refuse for moral reasons.

I hope that these observations may help to clarify some of the issues raised by Porter, Noonan, and Wright. I believe that their analyses, in particular those of Noonan and Wright, are seriously erroneous and trivialize the teaching of *Humanae vitae*, a teaching that definitely is, as Noonan rightly observed, "a given of Church doctrine."

NOTES

[1] Lawrence Porter, O.P., "Intimacy and Human Sexuality: A Challenge to the Consensus on Contraception," *Communio* 7.3 (Fall, 1980): 269-277.

[2] John T. Noonan, Jr., "Natural Law, the Teaching of the Church, and the Regulation of the Rhythm of Human Fertility," *American Journal of Jurisprudence* 25 (1980): 16-37. John Wright, S.J., "An End to the Birth Control Controversy?" *America* (March 7, 1981): 175-178.

[3] Porter, *loc. cit.*, pp. 275-276.

[4] Cf., for instance, Charles E. Curran, "Moral Theology in the Light of Reactions to Humanae Vitae," in his *Transition and Tradition in Moral Theology* (Notre Dame, Ind.: University of Notre Dame Press, 1980), p. 29-59, esp. pp. 32-37.

[5] Cf., for instance, Anthony Kosnik et al., *Human Sexuality: New Directions in American Catholic Thought* (New York: Paulist, 1977), pp. 92-95, 116-117, in particular p. 127.

[6] Charles E. Rice, "Reducing *Humanae vitae* to a Symbolic Gesture," *The Wanderer* 114.21 (May 21, 1981): 1, 8.

[7] Noonan, *loc. cit.*, p. 16. Subsequent references to Noonan's essay will be given in parentheses in the text.

[8] Rice, *loc. cit.*, p. 8.

[9] Another claim by Noonan is that a woman who engages in loveless sex with her husband has a right to contracept. Noonan here illegitimately extends a teaching

implicit in the encyclical, namely that if an act of marital intercourse is *forced* on a spouse (cf. *Humanae vitae,* n. 13), in a way that might truthfully be regarded as "quasi-matrimonial rape," the wife could protect herself against unwanted consequences of this forced act by using contraceptives. In such instances she would not be contracepting because she does not consent to the intercourse. But Noonan's "clarification" on this matter is not at all proper. As Rice notes: "The Pope correctly indicates that a forced conjugal act is not an act of true love; but he does not say that every act lacking in true love is therefore forced and justifies defensive contraception." *Loc. cit.,* p. 8.

[10] Bertrand de Margerie, S.J., "Reflections on Some Aspects of *Humanae vitae* To Which Less Consideration Has Been Given," *Osservatore Romano*; English Edition May 25, 1978. See also Elisabeth Anscombe, *Contraception and Chastity* (London: Catholic Truth Society, 1976), pp. 20-23.

[11] Cf. Pope John Paul II, Address of January 9, 1980, "Revelation and Discovery of the Nuptial Meaning of the Body," in *The Original Unity of Man and Woman* (Boston: St. Paul Editions, 1981), pp. 106-112.

[12] Wright, *loc. cit.,* p. 175. Subsequent references to Wrights' essay will be given in parentheses in the text.

[13] I am grateful to Professor Joseph M. Boyle, Jr., of the Center for Thomistic Studies in the University of St. Thomas in Houston for pointing out this fallacy to me.

7.
Sterilization: Catholic Teaching and Catholic Practice

In previous chapters we have examined the meaning of responsible parenthood, the crucial moral difference between periodic continence or natural family planning and contraceptive intercourse as ways of regulating conception, and the malice of contraception. In this chapter our consideration will focus on sterilization, more specifically, contraceptive sterilization, that is, sterilization undertaken precisely in order to prevent conception.

Contraceptive sterilization today is becoming more and more widespread in our society. Many resort to it because it has a lower "failure" rate than other methods of contraception and does not share the unpleasant side-effects of some of these other methods, although it, too, has some unpleasant side-effects.[1] It is quite frequently employed when the mother's health may be seriously jeopardized by another pregnancy or when the child-to-be may be seriously crippled by a genetically or chromosomally induced disease. In such instances it is alleged by many, including some Roman Catholic theologians, to be the most efficient, medically sound, and humane way for meeting parental and family responsibilities.

The authentic teaching of the Church, as is well known, holds that both contraception and "direct," that is, contraceptive sterilization are inherently wicked and that therefore no one may, for any reason whatsoever, practice contraception or undergo direct sterilization. This teaching has been reaffirmed over and over again by the magisterium. For instance, in his "Address to Italian Midwives" in 1951 Pope Pius XII said: "Direct sterilization—that is, the sterilizatin which aims, either as a means or as an end in itself, to render childbearing impossible—is a grave violation of the moral law."[2] He likewise made it clear that this was simply an extension of the Church's teaching on the immorality of contraception. Then in 1968, in *Humanae vitae*, Pope Paul VI, after showing why contraception must be repudiated, affirmed that "equally to be excluded . . . is direct sterilization, whether perpetual or temporary, whether of the man or of the woman."[3]

Despite these firm teachings of the magisterium, pressure was exerted to modify the position of the Church. Despite this pressure the bishops of this country, in releasing *The Ethical and Religious Directives for Catholic Health Facilities* in 1971, firmly taught that contraceptive sterilization is immoral.[4] But again pressure was applied by dissenting theologians, and the bishops of this country raised the issue once more for the Holy See to study. In reply the Sacred Congregation of the Faith firmly said:

> Any sterilization which of itself—that is, of its own nature and condition—has the sole immediate effect of rendering the generative faculty incapable of procreation is to be considered direct sterilization, as the term is understood in the declaration of the pontifical magisterium. . . . Therefore, notwithstanding any subjectively right intention of those whose actions are prompted by the cure or prevention of physical or mental illness which is foreseen or feared as a result of pregnancy, such sterilization remains absolutely forbidden according to the doctrine of the Church.[5]

And in 1980 the National Conference of Catholic Bishops released a "Statement on Tubal Ligations," once more clearly and firmly expressing the mind of the Church on the subject of contraceptive sterilization.[6] Finally, in *Familiaris Consortio* Pope John Paul II again rejected contraceptive sterilization, along with contraception, as immoral.[7] There can then be absolutely no question regarding the teaching of the Church on this subject.

Still theological dissent continues, and with it the pressure to change the teaching and practice of the Church. The reasoning employed by Bernard Häring is typical. According to him

> whenever the direct preoccupation is responsible care for the health of persons or for saving a marriage (which also affects the total health of all persons involved), sterilization can then receive its justification from valid medical reasons. If, therefore, a competent phsyician can determine, in full agreement with his patient, that in this particular situation a new pregnancy must be excluded now and forever because it would be thoroughly irresponsible, and if from a medical point of view sterilization is the best possible situation, it cannot be against the

principles of medical ethics, nor is it against 'natural law' (*recta ratio*).[8]

Richard A. McCormick, who makes Häring's position his own,[9] argued, in an article published after the firm declaration of the Sacred Congregation of the Faith in 1976, that this authoritative statement simply asserted that contraceptive sterilization was contrary to the moral good of the person and hence intrinsically evil and did not show that it is so; he likewise argued that this statement simply dismissed existing theological dissent, which he regarded as basically simply an alternative theological position to that of the Congregation, without critically assessing that dissent.[10] Häring's views are likewise shared by John P. Doyle, a priest on the faculty of the religion department of Iowa University,[11] by Charles E. Curran, the well known moralist at The Catholic University of America,[12] and by a sizable number of other theologians both in the United States and elsewhere. McCormick even claims that this position is "that of those whom I consider to be the most reputable and reliable theologians in the Church today."[13]

There is little wonder, then, that the issue of sterilization is one of the utmost urgency, particularly for those charged with the administration of Catholic hospitals. They are faced, on the one hand, with the authoritative teaching of the Church, and on the other hand with the position of a significant and influential body of theologians.

What I propose to do here is to offer some reflections on three interrelated issues: (1) the moral meaning of sterilization; (2) the question of theological dissent; and (3) the policy to be adopted by those in charge of Catholic health facilities. In conclusion I will offer some thoughts about the significance of this problem as a human and pastoral question.

1. The Moral Meaning of Sterilization

The Church teaches that contraceptive sterilization is an intrinsically evil act insofar as it attacks the moral good of the person. Here I will seek to show why this teaching of the Church is true. Before advancing my argument, however, I must point out that my efforts to do so will not be convincing to McCormick and the dissenting theologians and others who agree with his moral theory. Therefore, it may be useful, first, to review this moral theory.

McCormick has advanced and developed this theory, which he finds in the writings of many contemporary Catholic theologians, in a series of his influential "Notes on Moral Theology" for the journal *Theological Studies*.[14] He likewise has developed it in his 1973 Pere Marquette Theology Lecture, *Ambiguity in Moral Choice*,[15] and in his contribution to the volume *Doing*

Evil to Achieve Good,[16] in which he somewhat modified the position but in no way changed its basic norm, namely, that it is morally right deliberately to choose to do evil (in the sense of "premoral," "nonmoral," or "ontic" evil) for the sake of a proportionately greater ("premoral," "nonmoral," or "ontic") good.

Central to this theory is the distinction between moral good and evil and what is variously termed "premoral," "nonmoral," and "ontic" good and evil. By moral evil is meant sin, in the formal sense of a choice that one believes is morally wicked, and by moral good is meant the moral goodness of the agent. Advocates of this kind of moral reasoning agree that it is *always morally* wrong to intend moral evil or the sin of another. They likewise agree that it is *always morally* evil to intend an act described in such a way that it is known to be morally evil, that is, when it includes an evaluative term. Thus they would agree that it is *always morally* wrong to intend *murder* (defined as the unjust taking of human life).[17]

Moreover, in his recent writings[18] McCormick, and with him Philip S. Keane (another advocate of this type of moral reasoning),[19] is willing to grant that some sorts of actions can be so described that they include, within their description, a *disproportionate* reason for doing "premoral" evil. For example, McCormick would agree that it is *always morally* wrong to undergo sterilization simply to avoid a pregnancy because one wishes to play tennis.

"Premoral" ("nonmoral" or "ontic" in the language of some advocates of this position) good and evil, on the contrary, refer simply to basic goods of human persons such as life itself and health, friendship, knowledge and truth, peace and justice, etc.[20] According to these theologians we are, of course, to pursue such goods and to avoid their contraries (the "premoral" evils, evils such as death, disease, enmity, ignorance and falsehood, etc.) to the extent possible. Yet, they hold, there are times when these goods may come into conflict and it may not be possible to preserve all of them. The question thus arises: when is it morally legitimate to "do" evil, that is, to bring evil about? Traditionally, in Roman Catholic thought, such conflict situations were governed by the "principle of double effect." As this principle was understood by earlier theologians one could rightfully cause evil through an act of choice if, and only if, four conditions were verified: (1) the act itself, prescinding from the evil caused, is good or at least indifferent; (2) the good effect of the act is what the agent intends directly, only permitting or "indirectly intending" the evil effect; (3) the evil caused must not be the means to the good effect; and (4) there must be some proportionately grave reason for permitting the evil effect to occur.[21]

What McCormick and other proponents of "proportionalism" or "proportionalistic consequentialism" in effect do is reduce the principle of double effect to the principle of proportionate reason. For them it is the decisive criterion of the morality of choices and actions entailing the doing of "premoral" evil.[22] They thus argue that there are no intrinsically evil acts in the moral sense if the acts in question are described in morally neutral terms or in merely descriptive terms. Thus they argue, for example, that it is *usually wrong* to choose to kill an innocent person,[23] but that the choice to kill an innocent person (or to intend directly *any* "premoral" evil) can be morally good if there is a proportionately grave reason, i.e., if there is some proportionately greater good that can be fostered by the deliberate intent to set aside, impede or destroy this innocent human life (or some other "premoral" good).

Applying this theory to the issue of contraceptive sterilization, the advocates of proportionalism argue, as we have seen Häring do, that the good (again, I must note, a "premoral" good) of the whole well-being of the family justified the choice to do the "premoral" evil of sterilization.

Here I am not interested in criticizing this moral theory. Some of the basic objections to it were raised in Chapter 5, in the discussion of contraception,[24] and it has been, in my judgment, devastatingly criticized by such writers as Germain G. Grisez and John M. Finnis.[25] Obviously, if this moral theory were true, then one could never show that an act of contraceptive sterilization is intrinsically evil, just as it could never be shown that the act of killing innocent human persons or that of suicide is intrinsically evil. All one can do is to argue whether a reason assigned to justify such intentional acts of doing evil is in truth "proportionate," and reasonable people will obviously disagree over what constitutes a "proportionate" good, something evident in the disagreement between McCormick and Daniel C. Maguire over acts of "choosing death" for a suffering dying person.[26]

I will therefore proceed on the assumption that the moral theory of McCormick and those whom he regards as the "most reputable and reliable theologians of the Church" is false. Alternative moral theories, ones compatible with the teaching of the Church, exist.

One alternative, and the one in terms of which I hope to give good reasons to show that contraceptive sterilization is intrinsically wicked, is reflected today in the writings of such Catholic writers as Grisez, Finnis, Elisabeth Anscombe, and (I believe) Karol Wojtyla (Pope John Paul II).[27] It is a moral theory rooted, moreover, in the thought of St. Thomas Aquinas.[28]

On this theory there are basic fundamental goods of the human person, goods that contribute to the flourishing of human persons and human communities. Taken together, these goods go to make up the total human good, and among them are the goods of life and health, truth and knowledge, friend-ship, peace and justice, and practical reasonableness itself.[29] These are all goods *of* persons, not goods *for* persons; they are goods that human per-sons *prize* rather than *price*. As goods *of* persons, they participate in the goodness of the human person, the irreplaceable and precious image of God Himself.

Moral goodness enters in when we relate our person (or, to use a biblical expression, our "heart") to these goods, and we relate our person to them in and through our choices and actions.

The person whose heart is open to God is the one who is open to these human goods and to their realization in human persons, himself and others. None of these goods is the *summum bonum*, or an absolute good in the sense of being the be-all and end-all of human existence; only God is the *sum-mum bonum*. But a human person's moral or ethical good, his participation in the *Summum Bonum* or, as Vatican Council II put it, his acquired dignity as a person,[30] is totally dependent on his willingness to recognize these real goods of human person for what they are and to act responsbily in accord with his recognition of them for what they really are: real goods of human persons, created participations in the goodness of God Himself. Viewed religiously, these goods are gifts of our loving Father. They are the goods which, as Vatican II again put it, we will find "transfigured" in the com-pleted kingdom of "truth and life, holiness and grace, justice, love and peace."[31]

Because they really are good they ought to be considered as such by human persons; they ought to be viewed as blessings, not as curses. Since none of these goods is the absolute good, the *Summum Bonum*, none ought to be regarded as such as made to function as the key to solving conflict situations; in short, none ought to be regarded as the "proportionate good" for whose sake we have a moral right to intend directly the destruction of any other human good.[32] Although we cannot be pursuing all of these goods all of the time, and although we may, in tragic instances, suffer the loss or destruction of these goods in ourselves and others when otherwise the struggle to preserve them or participate in them would of necessity cause us to set aside or destroy other real goods of human persons, we ought to be unwilling to set our wills against any one of them or to say, in effect, that any one of them is here and now not a good but an evil. Each of these goods, in other words, is what classically would be termed a *bonum honestum*, something good in itself and not a mere *bonum utile* or pragmatic good.

Our power to generate human life, our fertility, is a personal power.

It is a power that we have precisely in virtue of our sexuality, which, as Pope John Paul II so rightly affirms, "is by no means something purely biological, but concerns the innermost being of the human person as such."[33] This great good, this God-given gift, is moreover a power ordered to a good of transcendent value, the communication of life and love to a new human person.[34] It thus, as again Pope John Paul II clearly states, "by its nature surpasses the purely biological order and involves a whole series of personal values."[35]

In addition, this power to generate new human life is inherently related to another personal and sexual power, the power quite unique to human persons, namely, the power to enter into communion with another human person in sexual coition. For the generation of new human life is not an act of reproduction but one of procreation, one that brings into being not only a new human person made in the image of God but also fosters love of a special and unique kind—marital love—between the persons collaborating in the generation of human life.

Both of these human sexual powers are integral to the human person and participate in the goodness of the human person. Each of these powers is a blessing given to the human person by God. It is possible to abuse these powers, and we can morally bring them into exercise only under certain conditions. But as such these powers are good and ought to elicit from us a response of love and acceptance because they are integral to our humanity, to our personhood.[36]

Deliberately to choose to act in a way that negates the human sexual power to enter into communion with another person through sexual union is, on the theory operative here, inherently or intrinsically evil. To choose to unite coitally with one who is not one's spouse is to abuse this power; it is to lie, as Pope John Paul II put it in *Familiaris consortio*.[37] To choose to exercise this power, even with one's spouse, is likewise wrong if respect for the spouse is not present, as Pope Paul VI noted in *Humanae vitae*.[38]

Similarly, it is not in accord with *recta ratio* or with the natural law (despite Häring's superficial contentions in the passage already cited) to choose to set aside or destroy the procreative good. In contraceptive sterilization one is setting aside and destroying the great human personal and sexual power to give life. One is saying, in effect, that this power is here and now not a God-given gift, a blessing, but a curse, a disease. The choice to sterilize directly or contraceptively is one that is morally justifiable only if one regards the human power to procreate as a merely utilitarian good, a *bonum utile*, a power that is not good in itself but good only because it helps to serve other goods that are truly personal. But to regard the human personal power of giving human life in this way is to repudiate its inherent goodness; it is pragmatically to reduce it to a merely biological function, to a useful good whose *personal value* is totally determined by the consciously chosen ends toward which it can be directed. And it is precisely in this way that the dissenting theologians regard the human personal and sexual power to procreate. As we saw in Chapter Five, they consistently speak of it as a "reproductive function," sharply distinguishing it from the "personal" sexual power to unite coitally. Yet to regard our power to give life in this way is to advance a kind of gnostic dualism, one in which the personal is identified with what is consciously experienced and to devalue the bodily in our existence.

To summarize: man's moral good is constituted by his willingness to recognize the inherent goodness of those real human goods which, together, go to make the whole human good and to choose to act in ways that manifest his love for their goodness and for the *Summum Bonum* who is their origin and source. The morally upright person ought not to be willing to act in ways that set aside or destroy these human goods and in effect to declare them to be, here and now, non-goods. But the human power to generate new human life is an inherently human and personal power, participating in the goodness of the human person. Sterilization is an intentional act in which one deliberately sets out to destroy this great human and personal power. It is thus an act that of its very nature attacks the moral good of the human person and that is, consequently, intrinsically evil, incapable of being "made right" by extrinsic factors.

2. The Question of Theological Dissent

It is beyond doubt, as we saw in the introductory pages of this chapter, that very many Roman Catholic moral theologians dissent from the authoritative teaching of the Church, not only on contraception and contraceptive sterilization, but on many other moral issues. In the previous section we examined the most common argument advanced by these theologians to support their position, the one advanced by Häring and accepted by McCormick and writers in the proportionalistic school of thought. But it may be useful, in approaching the question of theological dissent, to examine briefly the line of thought pursued by Charles E. Curran in his essay in which he seeks to "refute" past teaching of the Church.[39] If this article is examined, we find that no arguments are really advanced to "refute" the teaching. There is the simple assertion that

those who accept artificial contraception [and sterilization] understand human sexuality in terms of its relationship to the individual person, to his spouse or family and to all of society. In the light of these multiple relationships the individual has stewardship over his sexuality and his reproductive functions [and] the right to intervene in these functions in the light of the multiple relationships.[40]

In Curran's assertion we discover, I believe, the key claim made by the dissenting theologians. It is an argument that looks upon human power to give life to a new human person as a "reproductive" function. It is an argument that sees the *personal* significance of human sexuality as exhausted by its "relational" dimension. It is, in brief, an argument that has *in principle* separated the unitive (relational) and procreative meanings of human sexuality, deeming the latter as merely biological, i.e., as subpersonal or subhuman, and considering only the other as personal and truly human.[41]

Curran's version of the argument, moreover, implicitly relies on the proportionalist methodology, and in this it resembles the line of reasoning employed in the so-called Majority Report of the Papal Commission on the Regulation of Births. As one writer has noted, "underlying the Commission's argument . . . is the notion that physical evil [another name for "premoral," nonmoral," or "ontic" evil] or a certain violence against physical nature, done in pursuit of human ends [that is, in pursuit of alleged higher goods of the person that function as proportionate reasons] is in accord with natural law."[42]

What is striking, in my opinion, is that the Roman Catholic champions of contraception and contraceptive sterilization continually reassert, *as if self-evidently true*, the type of argument advanced in the mid 1960's to change Catholic teaching. There is the constant refrain that the Catholic teaching, the teaching reaffirmed by Pope Paul VI and Pope John Paul II, is physicalistic and biological in nature, deriving a moral norm from the "physical structure of the act." This refrain persists, despite the fact that numerous authors, among them Elisabeth Anscombe, Germain G. Grisez, John Kippley, Robert and Mary Joyce and others,[43] have amply shown that this teaching, far from being physicalistic, is predicated upon a profound personalism. The dissenting theologians then argue that their own position is to be regarded as at least probable, so that Catholics "in doubt" about the matter are free to choose their position in place of that set forth by the authentic magisterium.[44]

To go thoroughly into the mater of theological dissent would take us too far afield.[45] Consequently, in appraising the worth of theological dissent with respect to the issue of contraceptive sterilization (and of contraception itself), I think it may suffice to apply the criteria that McCormick himself suggested some years ago. In speaking of the response that Catholics, including theologians, ought to make to authentic but noninfallible magisterial teachings (and, for the sake of argument, I will hypothesize that the teaching on contraception and contraceptive sterilization can be so classified[46]), McCormick said that the initial response might not be actual assent but "a kind of connatural eagerness to accept and adhere to this teaching," and that this connatural eagerness would be concretized in various ways. One concretization would be "a readiness to reassess one's own positions in the light of this teaching, an attempt to see if this teaching can be supported on grounds other than those presented."[47]

A survey of the literature shows little evidence that dissenting theologians have made strenuous efforts to reassess their own positions. There is evidence, however, that others who have reassessed their own views have concluded that their dissent was ill founded and that there are good reasons to support this teaching. I thus submit that McCormick's own criteria for "responsible dissent" on this issue have not been adequately met by dissenting theologians. In any case, their views can in no way be regarded as "probable." The teaching of the Church is "in possession" and carries a binding force that can be set aside only if it can be conclusively shown to be erroneous. Since the argument of the dissenting theologians have been effectively and decisively criticized by competent authors, and since good moral arguments have been set forth to support the teaching of the Church, the claim that dissenting views constitute a probable opinion remains just that, a claim. It is one that ought to be rejected.

The teaching of the Church on the intrinsic malice of contraceptive sterilization is, as I have sought to show in this section, true. It is required by the basic principles of morality, of the natural law, and it is rooted in a respect and love for the basic goods of human existence and of the flesh-and-blood human persons in which these goods are meant to flourish. This teaching serves as a sure norm for making good moral choices. In a special way it is the norm that must shape the policies of institutions, such as Catholic hospitals, which represent the Church to the general public. Thus in the following section I will discuss the matter of policy for Catholic hospitals on sterilization.

3. A Policy for Catholic Hospitals on Sterilization

Although the Church's teaching on contraceptive sterilization is quite clear and well known, and although it is embodied in the *Ethical and Religious Directives for Catholic Health Care Facilities* promulgated by the United States hierarchy,[48] the matter of public policy on the part of Catholic hospitals with respect to sterilization is one that is heatedly debated today.

The issue focuses on the sterilization of women, or tubal ligations. Such sterilizing procedures require hospitalization, in contrast to male sterilization or vasectomy, which can be done in the private office of a doctor. And the issue arises because the public served by Catholic hospitals includes large numbers of non-Catholics who believe that contraceptive sterilization is morally permissible (as well as sizable numbers, unfortunately, of Catholics who share this judgment). The claim is made that in our pluralistic society the right, particularly of these non-Catholics, to act in accord with their own conscientious judgment must be respected, particularly in view of the fact that in many instances Catholic hospitals are supported, at times to considerable extent, by public funds derived from taxpayers, many of whom regard the teaching of the Church on this question as erroneous. The issue becomes critical when the Catholic hospital is the only health care facility serving the surrounding population.

Naturally theologians who dissent form the teaching of the Church and those members of religious orders operating hospitals who agree with the dissenting theologians believe that Catholic hospitals *ought to be allowed* to provide the "service" of sterilization to those for whom it poses no moral problems.[49] But aside from the pressure exerted by this group, there is the additional consideration, one admitted by the letter of the Congregation for the Doctrine of the Faith,[50] and by theologians who accept the teaching of the Church, that individual Catholics and Catholic institutions can, under very precise conditions, cooperate *materially* in acts that are intrinsically evil, such as sterilization. To explain this requires a brief description of the difference between formal and material cooperation and the conditions under which material cooperation in evil is permissible.

In *formal* cooperation in the evil of others, one *intends* the evil that is done and participates in the evil-doing by advising, counseling, promoting, or condoning it. It is always wrong to cooperate formally in evil, and no Catholic or Catholic institution is justified in formally cooperating in *any* evil, including the evil of contraceptive sterilization.

Material cooperation, on the other hand, is a type of cooperation in which one does *not* intend the evil that others are doing but is only permitting or tolerating this evil for the sake of avoiding even more serious evils. Such cooperation can be either *immediate* or *mediate*. Immediate material cooperation is the actual doing of the evil one disapproves of and is thus morally equivalent to formal cooperation (e.g., material cooperation would be immediate if a physician, who himself recognizes that sterilization is evil, nonetheless performs the sterilization on a woman on the grounds that she needs his technical expertise). Such material cooperation is never permitted.

But mediate material cooperation in the evil of others (which theologians further divide into *proximate* and *remote* material) is permissible on the basis of the principle of double effect. Thus a Catholic and a Catholic hospital may at times materially cooperate in the evil of others (only permitting or tolerating and not directly intending the evil done) when only in this way can a great harm be prevented. Even in such material cooperation care must be taken that scandal is not given.[51] Thus, for example, an employee of a drug store that stocks contraceptives might materially cooperate in the evil of contraception by selling these products to customers if it is impossible for him or her to find other employment.

The issue then arises, is it possible that Catholic hospitals might at times, particularly when they are the only health care facilities available in a given geographical region, materially cooperate in the evil of sterilization and permit such operations (tubal ligations, remember) to be carried out on their premises? In theory—a theory that the Sacred Congregation for the Doctrine of Faith acknowledges—material cooperation is a possibility. Thus the question more precisely is this: are the existential conditions present which would justify the application of this theory?

In an earlier version of this essay[52] I argued that in some instances, e.g., where the Catholic hospital is the only medical facility "within reasonable distance of persons who for conscientious reasons believe that sterilization is the 'right' thing to do," "one can argue that the conditions exist in which a Catholic hospital can materially cooperate by providing space, equipment, and personnel [non-Catholics who themsleves believe sterilization is justifiable] for sterilization." I argued that the "grave cause" allowing such cooperation "would be a respect for the consciences of others and a desire to avoid even greater evils, such as public outrage and a climate in which the Catholic hospital could no longer bear witness to evangelical ideals in the care of the sick." I also insisted that care must be taken to avoid scandal and to let the public know that the hospital regards sterilization as truly immoral and is merely tolerating this evil to be done on its premises.

The position I outlined, fortunately, was challenged by Anthony Zimmerman, S.V.D.[53] After studying his criticisms (which, unfortunately, do not seem to acknowledge even the theoretical possibility of material cooperation) and thinking at more length on the issue, I agree with him that my justification for material cooperation in the evil of contraceptive sterilization by Catholic hospitals in this country was ill conceived and that the argument I employed could be applied to "justify" material cooperation in the even greater evil of abortion.[54] I have now concluded that the conditions for material cooperation in the evil of sterilization simply do not exist in our society.

My principal reason for reaching this conclusion is that the procedure in question is the tubal ligation of a woman, a very serious operation that requires hospitalization. If a non-Catholic couple wishes to avoid a pregnancy by resorting to the evil of sterilization, they have the choice, in this country, of having the male sterilized, and this can be done in a doctor's office without involving the hospital at all. Thus this couple's conscience would be respected by the Catholic hospital—for they could still sterilize their marriage by having the husband vasectomized—and they in turn would respect the conscience of the Catholic hospital, something to which the Catholic hospital, as an institution, is entitled.[55]

Another serious reason leading me to abandon my earlier position and concur with Zimmerman's judgment is the fact that, should Catholic hospitals, out of a desire to respect the conscientious judgment of non-Catholics, begin to permit sterilizations on the grounds that their cooperation is only "material," enormous pressures would then be applied, both by advocates of abortion and by Catholics who dissent from the authentic teaching of the Church, to have Catholic hospitals "permit" abortions for the same reasons.

A Catholic hospital has the very serious obligation to bear witness to the truths about human existence proclaimed by the Church. This obligation is particularly serious in our culture, so deeply influenced by secular humanism. In my judgment, Catholic hospitals would be setting aside this serious responsibility were they to adopt a permissive policy toward sterilizations. If they were to do so, many would perceive their "permission" of this evil as a sign that they looked upon the authoritative teaching of the Church not as a truth of crucial importance to human existence but rather as a "party line" unfortunately still upheld by the official teachers of the Church but already regarded as erroneous by "thinking" Catholics.

Thus in my judgment it is not possible in our culture to justify material cooperation by Catholic hospitals in the evil of sterilization.

Conclusion

In conclusion I wish to offer some reflections about the *apparent* harshness of the Church's teaching on contraception/sterilization, for I believe that one of the principal reasons why this teaching is not accepted is the erroneous belief that it imposes intolerable burdens upon the consciences of men and women who are struggling as best they can to make their marriages a success, to care for the children they already have, and to avoid irresponsible pregnancies. All of us, I believe, can appreciate the anguish that many couples experience.

Here we need recall, first of all, that the teaching of the Church on contraception/sterilization does not at all mean that married persons must never express their love in the marital act. This teaching is, as we have seen in previous chapters, rooted in a recognition of the beauty of the marital act, one that is open to life and love. It is rooted in the recognition that the marital act is made to be *non-marital* if spouses, in choosing coition, likewise choose to set aside *either* its unitive *or* procreative goods.[56] What the Church teaches is that married couples ought to choose this way to express their love only when in choosing to do so they can show reverence for the great human good of unitive-procreative sexuality.

A married couple faced with the judgment, to use Häring's words in his apologia for contraceptive sterilization, that "in this particular situation a new pregnancy must be excluded now and forever because it would be thoroughly irresponsible" can choose to meet this problem by contracepting, by sterilizing, by practicing periodic continence, or by completely abstaining from marital relations. Häring and other dissenting theologians argue that sterilization (usually the tubal ligation of the wife) and/or the use of effective contraceptives is the most humane way to meet their problem. The dissenting theologians contend that this is justified by the natural law and by a true respect for the human person. They claim that *their* position is personalistic and not physicalistic, whereas the Church's teaching is physicalistic, not personalistic.

I submit that the "personalism" of dissenting theologians is shallow in character and dualistic. It is predicated upon the contention that the procreative power to give human life is merely biological in itself and *becomes* personal when assumed into consciousness.[57] It seeks to meet truly human and personal problems by the panacea of contemporary technology. But it forgets that pills are harmful to the health of women and that sterilization, in particular tubal ligation (the usually recommended procedure), has its own serious health problems for the woman. Even if the tubes are ligated, there is some chance for pregnancy to occur, and if it does occur it will be a tubal pregnancy with its attendant woes, something that a woman doctor, Hannah Klaus, acidly noted in commenting on the position of McCormick.[58]

The couple in this predicament (and it is not limited to those for whom pregnancy would be irresponsible because of the mother's health or because of danger of very serious genetic harm to the child) can meet their problem by the use of periodic abstinence, and some may choose to meet it by total abstinence,[59] and in choosing either of these ways of meeting their difficulty they manifest a true love for one another and for the great goods associated with their sexuality.

The teaching of the Church on the subjects of contraception and sterilization, far from being the physicalism and biologism that it is accused of being by the dissenting theologians, is in truth grounded in profound personalism. It is rooted in the truth that human persons are bodily beings who
differ from all other bodily beings of our experience insofar as they are gifted
with intelligence and free choice. These bodily persons make or break their
lives, give to themselves their own moral identity, by the choices they freely make. And the Church teaches that these bodily persons become truly
the persons they are meant to be when they choose in accord with a profound love for the real goods of human existence, and that among these goods
is the great good of procreative sexuality.

Thus the Church's teaching on the inherent malice of contracep-
tion/sterilization is by no means an intolerable burden placed on the consciences of men and women. It is rather a liberating truth rooted in an authentic
personalism, the kind of personalism so majestically developed by Pope John
Paul II in his writings.[60] It is a teaching intended to help us think seriously
about our lives as bodily, sexual persons who are called upon to love even
as we have been and are loved by God. As His living images we are asked
to open our hearts to the full range of human goods, the goods meant to
flourish in human persons, including the great good of the power of procreation, a power whereby God enables us to join with Him in the creation
of a new human life. And it is this good that is attacked, with direct intent,
in contraceptive sterilization.

NOTES

[1] In Chapter Five I noted the unpleasant side-effects of contraceptives, including serious health damage to women on the pill or using IUDs, the abortifacient effect of some alleged contraceptives, etc. On the undesirable side-effects
of sterilization see H. P. Dunn, M.D., "The Unexpected Sequelae of Sterilization," *International Review of Natural Family Planning* 1.4 (1977) 318-321.

[2] Pope Pius XII, "Address to Midwives," October 29, 1951. Text in Odile
Liebard, ed., *Official Catholic Teachings: Love and Sexuality* Wilmington, N.C.:
A Consortium Book from McGrath Publishers, 1978), n. 291, p. 110.

[3] Pope Paul VI, *Humanae vitae* n. 14.

[4] National Conference of Catholic Bishops, *Ethical and Religious Directives
for Catholic Health Facilities* (Washington, D.C.: United States Catholic Conference, 1971), nn. 18, 20.

[5] Sacred Congregation for the Doctrine of the Faith, *Documentum circa*

sterilizationem in nosocomiis catholicis, March 13, 1975. The English translation of this is given in *Origins: NC Documentary Service* 6 (1976) 33-35.

6 National Conference of Catholic Bishops, "Statement on Tubal Ligations," *Hospital Progress* 61.9 (September, 1980) 39.

7 Pope John Paul II, *Familiaris Consortio*, n. 30.

8 Bernard Häring, C.Ss.R., *Medical Ethics* (South Bend, In.: Fides, 1973), p. 90.

9 Richard A. McCormick, S.J., *How Brave a New World? Dilemmas in Bioethics* (New York: Doubleday, 1981), p. 273.

10 Ibid., pp. 260-268 (The essay in question originally appeared in *Theological Studies* 37 (September, 1976) 471-477.

11 John P. Boyle, *The Sterilization Controversy* (New York: Paulist Press, 1976), pp. 30-50.

12 Charles E. Curran, "Sterilization: Exposition, Critique, and Refutation of Past Teaching," in his *New Perspectives in Moral Theology* (Notre Dame, In.: University of Notre Dame Press, 1975), pp. 194-201.

13 McCormick, *How Brave a New World?*, p. 275.

14 McCormick developed the methodology of proportionalism in commenting on the positions of many influential theologians including Joseph Fuchs, Bruno Schüller, Louis Janssens, Peter Knauer, in his "Notes in Moral Theology" which regularly appear in the journal *Theological Studies* in the March issue of each year. The "Notes" for the years 1972, 1975, and 1977 are particularly important. In 1981 he collected his "Notes" over several years and published them in one large volume, *Notes on Moral Theology 1965-1980* (Washington, D.C.: University Press of America, 1981), and a study of the sections in this volume under the heading in the index of moral norms discloses the development of the theory. In the "Notes on Moral Theology" in *Theological Studies* 42 and 43 (1981, 1982) one will find continued presentation and development of this mode of moral reasoning.

15 *Ambiguity in Moral Choice* (Milwaukee: Marquette University Theology Department, 1973). This essay has since been published under the same title as the first chapter of *Doing Evil to Achieve Good*, ed. Richard A. McCormick, S.J. and Paul Ramsey (Chicago: Loyola University Press, 1978), pp. 7-53.

16 McCormick, "Commentary on the Commentaries," in *Doing Evil to Achieve Good*, pp. 193-267.

17 See, for example, McCormick, *Notes on Moral Theology 1965-1980*, pp. 644-645.

18 Thus, in "A Commentary on the Commentaries, " in *Doing Evil to Achieve Good*, McCormick at times speaks as though there were some actions, properly described, that would be intrinsically disproportionate. See, for instance, pp. 250-252.

19 Philip S. Keane, "The Objective Moral Order: Reflections on Recent Research," *Theological Studies* 43 (June, 1982), 260-278, at 269.

20 There is, I believe, fairly substantive agreement between McCormick and

the natural-law critics of proportionalism such as Germain G. Grisez, John M. Finnis and myself regarding the nature of the basic human goods. Here it is useful to compare McCormick, *How Brave a New World*, pp. 4-6 with Grisez, *Abortion: The Myths, the Realities and the Arguments* (New York: Corpus Books, 1970), pp. 312-313, and Finnis, *Natural Law and Natural Rights* (Oxford: Clarendon Law Series, Oxford University Press, 1980), pp. 85-90. As Grisez put it later, in a work he co-authored with Joseph M. Boyle, Jr., *Life and Death with Liberty and Justice: A Contribution to the Euthanasia Debate* (Notre Dame, In.: University of Notre Dame Press, 1978), p. 345, the type of proportionalistic/consequentialistic theory advocated by McCormick is, like the moral theory that he advocates and finds rooted in Aquinas, teleological or concerned with the true goods of human existence for the sake of which human persons make choices. Where the theories disagree is over the way in which we are to relate ourselves to these goods through our choices and actions.

[21] On the principle of double effect see Francis J. Connell, "Double Effect, Principle of," *New Catholic Encyclopedia* (New York: McGraw-Hill, 1967) 4. 1020-1022; William E. May, "Double Effect," *Encyclopedia of Bioethics* ed. Warren T. Reich (New York: Macmillan/Free Press, 1978) 1.316-320. For the history of this principle see Joseph T. Mangan, S.J., "An Historical Analysis of the Principle of Double Effect," *Theological Studies* 10 (1949) 341-361; J. Ghoos, "L'acte a double effet: Etude de theologie positive," *Ephemerides Theologicae Lovaniensis* 27 (1951) 30-52.

[22] This is quite clearly the position taken by McCormick, Keane, Daniel C. Maguire and other proportionalists. See McCormick, "Ambiguity in Moral Choice," in *Doing Evil to Achieve Good*, pp. 38-39 (pp. 77-79 of the 1973 Marquette Theology Department booklet); Keane, "The Objective Moral Order," pp. 267-268; Maguire, *Death by Choice* (New York: Doubleday, 1974), pp. 126-128.

[23] In her essay, "Teleology, Utilitarianism, and Christian Ethics," *Theological Studies* 42 (1981) 601-629, Lisa Sowle Cahill, herself a representative of this school of thought, seeks to defend McCormick in particular from criticisms. In the course of her article she suggests, p. 615, that the adjective "innocent" before the noun "life" in a proposition such as *one ought not to kill innocent human life* has moral, evaluative connotations. I believe that this analysis is idiosyncratic to Cahill.

[24] See Above, Chapter Five, Section II.

[25] Grisez, "Against Consequentialism," *American Journal of Jurisprudence* 23 (1978) 21-72; Grisez, *The Way of Our Lord Jesus Christ*, Vol. 1, *Christian Moral Principles* (Chicago: Franciscan Herald Press, 1983), Ch. 6; Finnis, *Natural law and Natural Rights* pp. 111-118.

[26] On this see McCormick, *Notes on Moral Theology 1965-1980*, pp. 441-443, where he entertains practical *doubts* about the *conclusions* reached by Maguire in his essay, "The Freedom to Die," in the August 11, 1972 issue of *Commonweal*, in which Maguire had argued that one can rightfully kill another mer-

cifully or kill himself for a proportionate reason. Maguire subsequently noted, in his *Death by Choice* p. 165, note 6, that there is this disagreement between himself and McCormick, a disagreement over a *conclusion* to be drawn by applying the method of proportionalistic analysis. But as Maguire goes on to note, both he and McCormick agree that the basic moral criterion is proportionate good.

[27] Grisez has developed his nonconsequentialistic theory of the natural law (one he holds is rooted in St. Thomas) in many works. Several of these have been listed in notes 20 and 25, above. In addition to these see the work he co-authored with Russel Shaw, *Beyond the New Morality* (2nd ed.: Notre Dame, In.: University of Notre Dame Press, 981). Finnis's basic work is that already mentioned, *Natural Law and Natural Rights*. Elisabeth Anscombe's thought is similar, but it has not been as deeply or extensively developed. See, however, the following; "Modern Moral Philosophy," in *Philosophy: The Journal of the Royal Institute of Philosophy* 33 (1958) 1-109; "War and Murder," in *Nuclear Weapons and Christian Conscience* ed. Walter Stein (London: Merlin Press, 1961); and her pamphlet *Contraception and Chastity* (London: Catholic Truth Society, 1977).

[28] The key Thomistic text is St. Thomas' discussion of the *many principles* (first principles) of the natural law in *Summa Theologiae*, 1-2, 94, 2. For a development of St. Thomas's teaching see my "The Meaning and Nature of the Natural Law in Thomas Aqiunas," *American Journal of Jurisprudence* 22 (1977) 168-189, and my essay, "The Natural Law and Objective Morality: A Thomistic Perspective," in *Principles of Catholic Moral Life*, ed. William E. May (Chicago: Franciscan Herald Press, 1981), pp. 151-192. An excellent study of St. Thomas, in which the terrible misrepresentation of his thought by dissenting proportionalist theologians is unmasked brilliantly, is that of Patrick Lee, "Permanence of the Ten Commandments; St. Thomas and His Modern Commentators," *Theological Studies* 42 (September, 1981) 422-443. See also my essay "Louis Jenssens, Thomas Aquinas, and the Meaning of Acts," *The Thomist* (October, 1984).

[29] On this, see above, note 20. Here it is also useful to note the human goods mentioned in the Preface for the Feast of Christ the King.

[30] *Gaudium et Spes*, n. 17: "Man attains [his] dignity when, liberating himself from all captivity to the passions, he pursues his end, in the free choice of good and procures for himself, effectively and by skillful effort, appropriate aids to that end." Translation of John M. Finnis in his superb article, "The Natural Law, Objective Morality, and Vatican II," in *Principles of Catholic Moral Life*, pp. 113-150.

[31] Ibid., n. 39.

[32] It can be shown, I believe, that the proportionalist method of making moral choices in fact erects certain kinds of human goods, in particular those *consciously experienced*, into absolutes requiring the destruction of what the proportionalists consider "lesser" goods (e.g., bodily integrity) whenever the continued flourishing of these bodily goods might inhibit participation in the consciously

experienced goods. This is another instance of the dualism at the heart of the "new Catholic morality." On this matter see my *Becoming Human: An Invitation to Christian Ethics* (Chicago: Franciscan Herald Press, 1974), Chapter Four.

[33] Pope John Paul II, *Familiaris Consortio*, n. 11.

[34] This, of course, is the truth constantly taught by the Church and by sound reason. For a marvelous development of it see Pope John Paul II, "The Nuptial Meaning of the Body," in *The Original Unity of Man and Woman* (Boston: St. Paul Editions, 1981), pp. 106-112.

[35] Pope John Paul II, *Familiaris Consortio*, n. 11.

[36] By sterilizing themselves, spouses *hold back* from one another something of themselves. On this see *Familiaris Consortio*, n. 32.

[37] Ibid., n. 11.

[38] Pope Paul VI, *Humanae vitae*, n. 13.

[39] On this see note 12, above.

[40] Curran, "Sterilization," p. 209.

[41] For a fuller analysis of this aspect of dissenting thought see my *Sex, Love and Procreation* (Chicago: Franciscan Herald Press, 1976) and Grisez, "Dualism and the New Morality," *Atti del Congresso Internazionale (Roma-Napoli 17/Napoli Aprile 1974) Thomaso d'Aquino nel suo Settimo Centenario*, vol. 5, *L'Agire Morale* (Napoli: Editioni Domenicane Italiane, 1977) pp. 323-330.

[42] Norbert Rigali, S.J., "The Historical Meaning of the *Humanae vitae* Controversy," *Chicago Studies* 15.2 (Summer, 1976) 127-139, at 131.

[43] See the following: Anscombe, *Contraception and Chastity;* Grisez, *Contraception and the Natural Law* (Milwaukee: Bruce Publishing Cmpany, 1964); John F. Kippley, *Birth Control and the Marriage Covenant* (Collegeville, Mn.: Liturgical Press, 1976); Mary Rosera Joyce, *Love Responds to Life* (Kenosha, Wi.: Prow Press, 1969); Robert Joyce, *Human Sexual Ecology* (Wshington, D.C.: University Press of America, 1980).

[44] This is the way McCormick argues in *How Brave a New World?*, pp. 273-278.

[45] Here it is important to note that prior to *Humanae vitae* Catholic theologians spoke of the right to withhold assent (nonassent) to noninfallibly proposed teachings of the magisterium, and not to any right to dissent. See, for example, F. A. Sullivan, S.J., *De Ecclesia* Vol. 1, *Quaestiones Theologiae Fundamentalis* (Romae: Apud Aedes Universitatis Gregorianae, 1963), p. 354; L. Salaverri, S.J., *De Ecclesia Christi*, in *Sacrae Theologiae Summa*, vl. 1, *Theologia Fundamentalis* ed. 5 (Matriti: B.A.C., 1952), p. 708, #669. I believe that theological *dissent* (as distinct from nonassent) can be justified *only if* the dissenter can show that any teaching is not compatible with basic truths proposed by the Church.

[46] With respect to contraception I believe that John Ford, S.J., and Germain G. Grisez have shown that this teaching has been *infallibly* proposed. See their article, "Contraception and Infallibility," *Theological Studies* 39 (1978) 258-312. I believe that a similar demonstration could be made of the teaching on contraceptive sterilization.

⁴⁷ McCormick, *Notes on Moral Theology 1965-1980*, p. 206.

⁴⁸ *Ethical and Religious Directives for Catholic Health Facilities*, nn. 18, 20.

⁴⁹ See, for instance, Charles E. Curran, *Issues in Sexual and Medical Ethics* (Notre Dame, In.: University of Notre Dame Press, 1977), pp. 150-158.

⁵⁰ This is the document referred to in note 5.

⁵¹ A brief, but competent, presentation of the principles governing material cooperation in evil is provided by Benedict Ashley, O.P. and Kevin O'Rourke, O.P., *Health Care Ethics: A Theological Analysis* (2nd. ed.: St. Louis: Catholic Hospital Assocation, 1982), pp. 191-193.

⁵² This appeared in *Homiletic and Pastoral Review* 77.11-12 (August-September 1977) 9-22.

⁵³ Anthony Zimmerman, S.V.D., "Sterilization for Contraceptive Purposes in Catholic Hospitals," *Homiletic and Pastoral Review* 78.10 (June, 1978); reprinted in *International Review of Natural Family Planning* 3 (Summer, 1979) 141-146.

⁵⁴ Here I must note that in using the term "greater evil" I am not using it in the sense in which this expression is used by the proportionalists. As both Grisez ("Against Consequentialism") and Finnis (*Natural Law and Natural Rights*, pp. 111-112) note, there is a legitimate sense in which one may use such expressions. This is so when the context is clearly nonmoral or *when the moral norm has already been established*. One makes a judgment that something is a "greater" good or evil within the framework provided by a moral norm. It is clear, too, that the attack on life itself is a greater attack on the good of life than an attack on bodily integrity. It is a "greater" evil to kill a person than it is to maim one. Yet it is evil to do either.

⁵⁵ Here it is worth noting that Paul Ramsey, the perceptive Princeton University moralist and outstanding Methodist, charges Catholic theologians, in particular Charles E. Curran, with seeking to take away from Catholic hospitals their right to an institutional conscience. He was speaking of the issue of abortion, not sterilization, but his remarks could well be extended to this subject too. He made his comments in reflecting on some essays of Curran in his splendid work, *Ethics at the Edges of Life* (New Haven: Yale University Press, 1978), p 82 ff.

⁵⁶ See above, pp. Chapter Four, Section 7.

⁵⁷ See above, pp. Chapter Five, Section II.

⁵⁸ Hannah Klaus, M.D., in a letter to the editor of *Hospital Progress* 61.11 (November, 1980).

⁵⁹ In an essay that I wrote to support the Bishops' "Statement on Tubal Ligation," (the essay was "Contraceptive Serilization: No Panacea for Human Problems," and appeared in *Hospital Progress* 61.9 (September, 1980). I noted that at times Catholic couples and others who recognized the malice of sterilization might "bite the bullet" and choose, perhaps because of psychological problems with periodic abstinence, to abstain completely from marital relations in order to meet their responsibilities. Francis X. Meehan, a priest-theologian at St. Charles Seminary in Philadelphia, thought that this would mean that the couple

would be acting against the marital good of unity or the unitive good of the marital act (cf. his essay, "Contemporary Theological Developments on Sexuality," in *Human Sexuality and Personhood* (St. Louis: Ppoe John XXIII Medical-Moral Center, 1981), pp. 173-190, at p. 181 and note 29, p. 189, or at least he suggested that if they did abstain one would wonder how they would honor this good of marriage. I find this strange. The marital act is a beautiful way of expressing conjugal love and of achieving unity in marriage, but married couples can express their love for one another in countless ways. There is a time to embrace, and there is a time not to.

[60] On this see the excellent work by Ronald Lawler, O.F.M. Cap., *The Christian Personalism of Pope John Paul II* (Chicago: Franciscn Herald Press, 1982).

8.
Reverence for Human Life
In Its Generation

In an unforgettable homily given to a great crowd assembled for Mass on the Capitol Mall in Washington, D.C., on October 7, 1979, Pope John Paul II eloquently proclaimed: "Nothing surpasses the greatness or dignity of a human person. Human life is not just an idea or an abstraction. Human life is the concrete reality of a being that lives, that acts, that grows and develops. . . . Human life is precious because it is the gift of a God whose love is infinite; and when God gives life, it is forever."[1]

In affirming the surpassing preciousness of human life the Holy Father was simply expressing the constant faith of the Church.[2] According to this faith, a human being, the concrete bodily being, male or female, endowed with human life, is a being of moral worth, a subject of inviolable and inalienable rights that are to be recognized by others and protected by the laws of society.[3]

Because human life is so precious, there is an obligation to revere it not only in its being but also in its coming-into-being.[4] The Church has always clearly taught the need for reverencing human life in its generation, and in his pastoral instructions to the American people Pope John Paul II summarized masterfully the principal elements of this teaching, particularly in his homily on the Mall. In that homily he provided us with a practical agenda for reflecting on this subject, "Reverence for Human Life in Its Generation." For in it he spoke of the beauty of marriage, that indissoluble covenant of life and love wherein *alone* human life can rightly be generated and given the home it deserves for its proper development. In it he strongly condemned the barbaric crime of destroying unborn human life, and he also alluded to the irresponsibility of contraceptive acts, which only two days before, in an address to the bishops of the United States, he had clearly repudiated as seriously wrong when he emphatically reaffirmed the constant teaching of the Church, the teaching that his predecessor Pope Paul VI had courageously upheld in *Humanae vitae*.[5]

Since the irresponsibility of contraception and its anti-life character have been discussed at length in the previous chapters of this work, what I propose to do in the present chapter is to show the truth of the following propositions. First, *human life can be rightly reverenced in its generation only when this life is begotten in an act that expresses the selfless and exclusive love of the spouses for each other*. Second, *the deliberate intention to destroy unborn human life through abortion is an infamous crime that must be legally proscribed*.

Before considering these propositions, however, there is a question of great practical importance that needs to be addressed, even if briefly. This is the relationship between a proper reverence for human life and "good law."

According to the faith of the Church so beautifully expressed by Pope John Paul II, human life is endowed with an inherent dignity and sanctity. As Paul Ramsey has noted perceptively, "The notion that an individual human life is absolutely unique, inviolable, irreplaceable, noninterchangeable, not substitutable, and not meldable with other lives is a notion that exists in our civilization because it is Christian." Professor Ramsey continued by saying, "and that idea is so fundamental to the edifice of Western law and morals that it cannot be removed without bringing the whole house down."[6]

The truth that every human being, the concrete bodily being endowed with human life, is a being of moral worth and the bearer of inviolable and inalienable rights is not, however, self-evident. This great truth is both a gift of divine revelation *and* an achievement of human intelligence insofar as it *can be* made manifest to the human mind.[7]

Yet it is not a truth that all people recognize. In fact, there is growing evidence that this notion of human life is losing its hold on the minds of contemporary men and women. At the beginning of the 1970's an editorial in *California Medicine* noted that "the reverence for each and every human life has . . . been a keystone of Western medicine. . . . This traditional ethic," the editorial continued,

> is still clearly dominant, but there is much to suggest that it is being eroded at the core and may eventually be abandoned. . . . It is not too early for our profession to examine this new ethic, recognize it

for what it is, and prepare to apply it in a rational development for
the fulfillment of mankind in what is almost certain to be a biologically oriented world society.[8]

Today, a little over a decade later, there is more reason to believe that this
"new ethic" to which the editorial referred, the "quality of life" ethic, has
actually become dominant in our culture and is reflected in the mores and
legal structures of our society.

The notions of the "sanctity of life" and of "the quality of life" are
speculative in character, and it does not lie within the competence of civil
government to determine which is true, nor can these notions be put into
human minds by legislative actions. Nonetheless, the *normative principles*
associated with these two differing and contradictory[9] notions of human life
are *not* speculative truths upon which reasonable people may disagree, but
are rather *practical* propositions or precepts that can be tested by what John
Courtney Murray called the "exigencies of civil conversation."[10]

Among the normative proposals advocated by adherents of the quality
of life ethic—and unfortunately these proposals are to be found in the writings
of several influential Roman Catholic writers[11]— are the following: (1) Only those members of the human species who are "meaningfully" alive and
not merely biologically so ought to be protected by law against homicide;[12]
and, (2) In determining whether a proposed act or practice is morally
justifiable one must assess its consequences and choose that act or practice
that will bring about the greater or proportionate good, even if the act or
practice is the sort that human agents cannot freely choose without having
the intent to do evil.[13] Among the normative proposals associated with the
sanctity of life ethic are the following: (1) Every living member of the human
species, being equal to all other members of this species in its humanity,
ought to be protected by law against homicide; and, (2) one ought not to
choose freely to do evil for the sake of good to come.[14]

If these normative proposals are closely examined, one will discover,
I believe, that those associated with the quality of life ethic conflict with
more basic requirements of practical reasonableness,[15] such as *good is to
be done and pursued and evil is to be avoided*, and *one ought not to do
unto others as one would not have them do unto oneself*,[16] whereas the normative proposals associated with the sanctity of life ethic meet these basic
requirements. In short, the moral priciples or requirements of practical
reasonableness in terms of which the normative proposals listed can be tested
for their truth or falsity are themselves self-evidently true, in the sense that
they can be recognized immediately by any rational agent as undeniable requirements of purposeful human activity and do not have to be shown to

be true on the basis of anything prior to themselves.[17] These principles, and the norms that can be shown to be compatible with them,[18] constitute what Murray called "good law," insofar as they are "invested not with the sanctity that attaches to dogma but only with the rationality that attaches to law."[19] These principles are simply the human expression of what Vatican Council II called "the highest norm of human life," namely, "the divine law itself— eternal, objective, and universal, by which God orders, directs, and governs the whole world and the ways of the human community according to a plan conceived in his wisdom and love."[20]

It is not possible to pursue this vitally important matter farther here. My principal reason for introducing it is to combat any sense of political impotence that may threaten those who steadfastly shape their lives by the wonderful truth that human life is indeed a precious gift of God and therefore endowed with surpassing dignity and sanctity. It would be wrong, and would violate the basic principles of practical reasonableness, to compel our fellow citizens to assent to the truth that human life is sacred. But even if this truth is not formally acknowledged, it is still possible to protect human lives in their being and in their coming into-being by "good law" rooted in the basic requirements of practical reasonableness. They can be so protected because the basic principles of practical reasonableness, the "exigencies of civil conversation" upon which a just political order depends, can be shown to demand that free and morally upright citizens, no matter what their differences on speculative questions, be willing to regard justice and due process of law as exigent for others, even those whom they merely recognize as fellow humans, fellow members of the same species, as they are for themselves and those whom they hold dear.[21]

1. Marriage, the Generation of Human Life, and the Irreverence for Human Life Manifested in Its Reproduction by Non-marital Means

In his homily on the Mall Pope John Paul II said that human life is precious not only because it is a gift from a loving God but also because "it is the expression and the fruit of love." Continuing, he said, "This is why life should spring up within the setting of marriage."[22]

Most people would agree with Pope John Paul on this. It is true, unfortunately, that many lives do come to being in the wombs of mothers who are not married to the men who have impregnated them; but this is almost universally regarded as a tragedy, and rightly so.[23] It is a tragedy not because a new human life has come into being, but because this life, this being filled with human potential and "capable of love and of service to humantiy,"[24] is beginning life in conditions that are unjust both to it and to its mother.

What is even more tragic today is that many people who agree that children ought not be conceived by women who are not married to the men who impregnate them believe that the proper way to remedy the situation is to provide these women with contraceptives and, should contraception "fail," abort the human life that has been conceived.[25]

Despite the widespread agreement that children ought to be generated by married couples and not out of wedlock, there are some in our society who urge that "responsible" single persons (of either sex) or couples consenting to live together (whether of the opposite or same sex) be recognized as having a right to give life to a new human being (either through heterosexual coition or through other generative procedures now available) so long as they are willing to give this life nurture and education. In addition, some urge that not every married couple has a right to have children, suggesting that marriage is not of itself a sufficient criterion for parenthood and that some further test be established and met before married persons can be considered to have a right to procreate.[26]

It is not possible here to address the issues that these groups raise, although I think that the evidence and arguments needed to respond effectively to them will be substantively contained in the analyses that will subsequently be given of proposals to generate human life non-maritally.

Of more immediate and pressing concern here are the views of those who think that married couples may, if necessary, rightly make use of such technologies as artificial insemination and in vitro fertilization in order to generate new human life. What I propose to do now is to examine their reasoning and to show that any attempt to generate human life non-maritally, whether by artificial insemination, in vitro fertilization, cloning or any other possible means, is wicked and unjust, an act of irreverence for human life in its generation. In what follows I will limit my discussion to in vitro fertilization, for once it is seen why this mode of generating human life is wrong one will also see why it is wrong to choose to generate human life through artificial insemination, whether by vendor[27] or by use of sperm provided by the woman's husband, and cloning.[28] I will further limit the discussion by restricting it to a consideration of in vitro fertilization by *married* couples.

A. What In Vitro Fertilization Is

In vitro fertilization is the name given to the act of generating human life in the laboratory by fertilizing a human ovum, taken from the body of a woman by a procedure known as laparoscopy, with human sperm provided by a male. The being brought into existence by this process is then nurtured at first in the laboratory until it reaches the stage of development when it can be implanted in a human womb where, it is hoped, it will undergo intrauterine development until normal birth.

The first child to be born after being conceived in this manner was Louise Brown. It is worth noting that she was born on July 25, 1978, the tenth anniversary of Pope Paul VI's encyclical on marriage, *Humanae vitae*, in which he affirmed that there is an indissoluble bond willed by God and not to be deliberately sundered by human choice between the unitive or love-giving and the procreative or life-giving meanings of human sexuality.[29] The significance of Pope Paul's teaching for a proper moral assessment of in vitro fertilization and other modes of "artful childmaking"[30] will be of central concern to us later.

In Louise Brown's case the same woman provided the ovum and subsequently nurtured in her womb the developing human life and, after birth, continues to act as Louise's mother. Moreover, the sperm used to fertilize Mrs. Brown's ovum was provided, through masturbation, by her husband. But I should note that various permutations and combinations of this mode of generating human life are possible. Thus different women could (a) provide the ovum, (b) nurture the developing human life within the womb, and (c) act as the child's mother after birth; and the sperm used to fertilize the ovum could be taken from a male other than the spouse of the woman from whom the ovum is taken or the woman(en) who would bear and/or raise the child. But as noted already, I will in what follows limit discussion of this mode of artful childmaking to its use by married couples.

B. Purposes of In Vitro Fertilization

Richard A. McCormick, S.J., has noted that there are two generic purposes that "reproductive interventions" such as in vitro fertilization might serve. The first he calls individual or personal purposes, and by this he means that a reproductive intervention is used to enable a couple childless because of some physical cause to have a child of their own. Thus in the case of Louise Brown the purpose was to alleviate the couple's infertility caused by her mother's blocked fallopian tubes. The second generic purpose, McCormick noted, is eugenic, either positive or negative.[31] Although a few scientists have championed the use of reproductive interventions for positive eugenic purposes, McCormick pointed out that the majority of scientists reject this possibility as utterly unworkable and even dangerous.[32] He did not, however, comment at any length on the possible negative eugenic purposes that reproductive interventions such as in vitro fertilization might serve. I would therefore like to suggest some. Although these are not possible today, they are not in principle unworkable and may, given sufficient technologcial progress, be feasible in the future.

We know, for example, that a married couple, each of whom is the bearer of some recessive genetic defect (e.g., Tay-Sachs disease), runs a twenty-five percent chance of conceiving a child who will actually be crippled by this terrible disease should they choose to generate life through the marital act. It may perhaps be possible to remove ova, examine them to determine whether they bear the genes responsible for the disease in question, destroy those that do carry these genes, and then fertilize in vitro an ovum free of them with the husband's sperm, implanting the developing child in her womb where it can be nurtured until birth. A child generated in this way would definitely not run the risk of being actually afflicted with the genetically induced disease, although he or she might, like his or her parents, be a carrier of the disease should the sperm used to fertilize the ovum bear the genes in question. Should it be possible to identify sperm as well as ova carrying the genes responsible for the disease and separate them from sperm free of such genes, it would then be possible to generate a child not only free from the disease but not even the carrier of genes responsible for causing it.

C. Arguments Used to Justify the Use of In Vitro Fertilization for Married Couples

There are two major arguments used to justify resort to in vitro fertilization. One justifies use of in vitro fertilization not only by married couples, otherwise childless, who seek to have a child of their own, but also by non-married couples and individuals. This broad argument likewise is used to justify vendor insemination and other modes of the laboratory generation of human life. The second major argument is more cautious and is intended exclusively to justify the resort to in vitro fertilization by married couples who otherwise cannot have a child of their own.

The first argument is advanced by such writers as Joseph Fletcher, Robert Francoeur (a former priest who teaches biology at Fairleigh Dickenson University), and Michael Hamilton.[33] The form in which this argument is given by Fletcher merits attention both because it summarizes the type of reasoning employed by all who welcome the advent of artful childmaking and because in it we can discern the major presuppositions underlying the argument. Fletcher put it as follows:

> Man is a maker and selector and a designer, and the more rationally contrived and deliberate anything is, the more human it is. Any attempt to set up an antinomy between natural and biological reproduction, on the one hand, and artificial or designed reproduction, on the

other, is absurd. The real difference is between accidental or random reproduction and a rationally willed or chosen reproduction. . . . If it [the latter] is "unnatural," it can only be so in the sense that all medicine is. . . . It seems to me that laboratory reproduction is radically human compared to conception by ordinary heterosexual intercourse. It is willed, chosen, purposed, and controlled, and surely these are among the traits that distinguish *homo sapiens* from others in the animal genus. . . . Genital reproduction is, therefore, less human than laboratory reproduction, more fun, to be sure, but with our separation of baby making from love making, both become more human because they are matters of choice, not chance.[34]

Several features of this truly Orwellian argument merit critical commentary. Note first that Fletcher regards the generation of human life as an act of reproduction; babies are entities that we "make." They are, as it were, products of our artisitc creativity, and since these "products" can be more deliberately "designed" and "planned' by the use of various techniques of artful childmaking than they can be by the "random" selection of what Fletcher elsewhere calls "reproductive roulette,'[35] it follows, according to him, that it is more human to "make" them in a controlled and designed way than to "make" them haphazardly. The notion that a child is a "product" is one to which I shall return.

Note secondly Flether's concept of human intelligence. He evidently considers human intelligence as primarily a "technical reason," that is, the capacity to plan and organize and arrange means efficiently to reach predetermined goals.[36] Although this is one aspect of human intelligence—it is what helps us make efficient use of our time, "control" nature and create the world of art and culture—it is surely not the only aspect of intelligence. What Fletcher does is equate human intelligence with but one of its operations, namely its artistic, creative one, and to ignore other crucially important intellectual operations, in particular its speculative capacity to discover the truth about reality and its practical capacity to put order into our moral lives by directing choice according to objective norms.[37]

Finally, note Fletcher's contention—one, I believe, shared by many in our culture—that there is nothing morally problematic in our ability to sever completely the bonds linking the unitive, amative, or "love-making" (better, "love-giving") meaning of our genital sexuality and its procreative or, as Fletcher has it, its "reproductive" or "baby-making" aspect. Here Fletcher expresses agreement with Ashley Montagu and others who contend that "it is necessary to be unequivocally clear concerning the distinction between *sexual* behavior and *reproductive* behavior."[38] They are, Fletcher alleges, radically different sorts of human activity, governed by completely different norms. Since in vitro fertilization and other forms of artful childmaking require the intentional choice to sever the bond between the unitive and propagative meanings of a human person's genital sexuality, this is evidently a central issue, one to which I shall return.

Commenting on the position advanced by Fletcher and others of similar mind, McCormick observed that it rests on three assumptions: (1) a "consequentialistic or teleological[39] normative position," according to which an act or practice is right and good "if, on balance, it does more good than harm and helps to minimize human suffering"; (2) a sharp distinction (one I have already noted) "between sexual love and the generation of human life"; and (3) a conception of parenthood "as a relationship essentially and principally defined by acts of nurturing, not by acts of begetting."[40]

I call attention to McCormick's comments for several reasons. First, they call to our attention two features in this position—its consequentialism and its understanding of parenthood—that were not explicity brought out in the passage from Fletcher analyzed previously. And the features McCormick notes help expalin why the reasoning employed justifies not only in vitro fertilization by married couples but also all sorts of reproductive interventions.

Secondly, McCormick's comments will help us grasp the presuppositions behind another position, one more cautious and nuanced than that advocated by Fletcher and his colleagues, that is used to justify in vitro fertilization when this is limited to helping *married* couples, otherwise childless, have a child of their own. I will now examine this position, one that McCormick himself and some other Roman Catholic theologians who challenge Church teaching on contraception, steriliztion, and other matters accept.

Its general contours are well described by McCormick. Thus it will be helpful, in initiating discussion of it, to see how he expresses its underlying assumptions. McCormick writes, in speaking of the underlying presuppositions of those who advance this argument to justify in vitro fertilization for married couples, as follows:

> First, they are not pure teleologists [by this he means consequentilistic teleologists, (cf. note 39)] in their moral thinking—that is, they argue that factors other than consequences need to be taken into account in offering a valid ethical evaluation of any human act, *although many such writers do believe that a proportionately good enough end can justify the deliberate, direct intent to effect some kinds of disvalues and evils* [emphasis added]. Second, they maintain that a meaningful and reciprocal relationship between sexual love and the generation of human

life exists and that it is no mere evolutionary accident that human life comes into existence through an act that is also capable of expressing love between a man and a woman. Third, while recognizing that acts of nurturing life are distinct from acts of generating life and that acts of nurturing are included within the meaning of parenthood, they also affirm that acts of generating life are parental in nature and carry with them responsibilities for nurturing the life procreated.[41]

McCormick has here ably set forth the basic presuppositions shared by several authors, including such Roman Catholics as Johannes Gründel, Charles E. Curran, and McCormick himself, [42] who have come to the conclusion that in vitro fertilization when restricted to helping married persons *can be* a morally good choice when other conditions are also fulfilled. These writers also, it can be noted incidentally, hold that husband artificial insemination is morally justifiable.

Before offering critical observations on the presuppositions of these authors, I wish to call attention to some of the "other conditions" that must be met, in the judgment of these authors, if in vitro fertilization for married couples is to be morally acceptable.

One of the most important other conditions that must be met is that serious harm to the child-to-be-begotten from this procedure itself must be reasonably excluded. These writers recognize that in vitro fertizliation is a medical experimentation upon a human subject—in this case the child-to-be—and that it is morally wrong to expose this subject to serious and unknown risks in order to satisfy the desires of its parents.

Their concern here is prompted by the very serious objections to in vitro fertilization raised intially by Paul Ramsey and Leon Kass.[43] Thus to understand their position it is important to grasp properly the significant moral question posed by Ramsey and Kass. I shall present the question in the form given to it by Ramsey in his argument against *any* effort to generate human life by in vitro fertilization.

To understand Ramsey's argument it is imperative to be clear about a crucial matter. The human subject with whose well-being Ramsey is concerned, in making his argument, is the child-to-be in the sense of the child who will eventually be born as a result of the procedure. In advancing his argument Ramsey wanted to prescind from the question of the moral status of the living being existing here and how in the laboratory petri dish after fertilization or of the developing unborn being in the mother's womb after successful implantation. The subject upon whom Ramsey claims that an unethical experimentation is being done is thus *not* the living being existing in the laboratory after fertilization (and that may be "discarded" prior to implantation should any discernible abnormality develop), nor is it the living being in the mother's womb that may be aborted should amniocentesis disclose that it may possibly be afflicted with a serious malady. Rather the subject of the unethical experimentation in Ramsey's argument is the child-to-be born, the child who is *not yet* in being after fertilization and during pregnancy but who will be in being after delivery.

Ramsey argued that in vitro fertilization is an unethical experimentation on *this* human subject *"unless* the *possibility* of irreparable damage to this child-to-be can be definitively excluded." He then argued that "this condition cannot be met, at least not by the first 'successful cases.' "[44] By this he meant that this condition has not even now been met, even after the birth of Louise Brown and a few other children, apparently normal. It has not been met because we do not know *yet* whether some harm later to be suffered by these children in their lives may have been induced by the procedure itself.

To put it briefly, Ramsey claimed that researchers simply cannot *"exclude* the possibility that they will do irreparable damage to the child to be."[45] They cannot know, *nor can they ever come to know*, what possible harm they are doing to this possible child *without being willing to inflict such damage in order to find out*.[46] And this, Ramsey insisted, is an irresponsible and unwarranted injustice to this child to be.

The defenders of in vitro fertilization by married couples recognize the serious question Ramsey posed. They nonetheless claim that his position is too stringent. Were it true, they say, then it would even be immoral for married couples to choose to have children through normal marital relations, insofar as they cannot absolutely exclude the possibility that the child they beget may be irrevocably and irreparably harmed in its coming-into-existence because of unknown recessive genetic defects or mutations.[47] They therefore claim that the moral question posed by Ramsey is better expressed in normative terms if we agree that one necessary condition that must be met prior to resorting to in vitro fertilization is the reasonable expectation that the risks to which the child to be will be submitted will be less than or equivalent to those that might be reasonably expected in normal generation though marital relations.[48] Whether or not this prior condition can be met is a matter that can only be settled by scientific data, and on this, at present, authorities are divided.[49]

Another condition that must be met, according to these authors, if in vitro fertilization is to be rightly used, is an unwillingness to abort a child conceived through this process and implanted in the mother's womb, should some abnormality develop. At least this is a condition that several of the authors adopting this position require. Many of these writers are also concerned about the problem of "discarding" fertilized ova (better, human lives in their very beginning) prior to implantation. Although most of the writers under consideration believe that individual personal life is not present prior to implantation or some later stage of development and that therefore the living beings here and now present in laboratory petri dishes prior to implantation are not personal subjects with a right to life in a strong sense, they are nonetheless concerned about the problem of "wastage" and of "discarded" zygotes (their moral sensibilites, in short, are much more developed than are Fletcher's and those who share his view). Thus many of the writers adopting this "more cautious" and "nuanced" defense of in vitro fertilization add as a further condition for its moral justification the stipulation that only one ovum from the mother be fertilized by her husband's sperm and that there be the intention to implant the resultant life within her womb so that it can be carried to term.[50]

I will forego comment on the issues raised by these "other conditions" so that attention can center on the basic underlying assumption of the authors who propose that in vitro fertilization, given the fulfillment of these conditions, may be rightly chosen by married couples as a way of fulfilling their desire for a child of their own so long as the wife's ovum is fertilized by her husband's sperm.

The third assumption of these authors, namely, that acts of generating life are parental and carry with them the responsibility to nurture the life generated, is surely correct. This assumption poses no problems. But what of the other two assumptions?

Although proponents of this position reject the kind of consequentialistic thinking employed by Fletcher (an out-and-out utilitarianism), they nonetheless do believe, as McCormick noted, "that a proportionately good enough end can justify the deliberate, direct intent to effect some kinds of disvalues and evils." I submit that these authors, while eschewing the simplistic utilitarian calculus of Fletcher, are nonetheless consequentialistic or "proportionistic" consequentialists in their normative ethical theory. They justify "exceptions" to the moral norms they develop (whether on consequentialistic or nonconsequentialistic grounds or a mixture of both) on the basis of a consequentialistic criterion, that, namely, of the alleged "greater good." With McCormick they allege that it is morally right to choose to do a ("premoral") evil for the sake of some greater ("premoral") good to come. In this instance, they are willing to choose to sever the bond uniting the intimate genital expression of marital love to the generation of human life—and they obviously believe that this bond is something good so that the choice to sever it is indeed the choice to do an evil or disvalue—because the choice to do *this* evil is ordered to the accomplishing of something they regard as an even greater good, namely, the generation of a child ardently desired by the couple. These authors thus subscribe to the consequentialistic proposal that *it is morally right to choose to do (premoral) evil for the sake of a proportionately greater (premoral) good.*

This basic normative presupposition has already been examined in previous chapters, so that there is no need here to repeat the criticisms made of it already.[51] It is, as we have already seen, a false proposition. It is a normative principle compatible with a "quality of life" ethic, one that denies that there are any truly absolutely inalienable rights of human persons[52] although conceding that some rights may be "practically absolute" insofar as it is diffciult to conceive of a proportionate good that might justify doing massive "premoral evils" destructive of human rights (e.g., executing a hostage).

The falsity of *this* assumption of the advocates of a "more cautious" defense of in vitro fertilization is of itself sufficient to show the fallaciousness of their argument. But in addition, another assumption made by these authors is erroneously understood by them and is so precisely because of their pro-portionalistic (as opposed to utilitarian) consequentialism and because of the dualism that their proportionalism engenders. They *rightly* assume, as McCormick tells us, that "a meaningful and reciprocal relationship between sexual love and the generation of human life exists and that it is no mere evolutionary accident that human life comes into existence through an act that is also capable of expressing love between a man and a woman [better, between a husband and wife]." They thus wish to keep the generation of human life within the marital covenant and to exclude the use of in vitro fertilization by nonmarried persons. They rightly see marriage, marital coi-tion, and the generation of human life as inherently interrelated,and they regard this as a human value.

Nonetheless, they conclude that the choice by married couples to resort to the laboratory generation of human life may be justified (under the con-ditions already noted) even though this choice does entail the intentional severing of the bond uniting the love-giving and life-giving meanings of genital sexuality and of the marital act. They hold, in short, that it is moral-ly acceptable to choose to generate human life by acts that are not those of marital coition but rather those of persons skilled in the employment of contemporary biological knowledge and technology. And they hold this precisely because they are consequentialistic in their methodology. Moreover, implicit in their justification of choosing to do the *evil* of severing the bond uniting the life-giving and love-giving meanings of the marital act is the claim that the good thus set aside—a good rooted in the bodily being of human persons—is less than the good achieved by the willingness to do this evil, the good, namely, of providing the couple with a child of their own. I submit that here is a latent dualism, an understanding of human existence that subordinates personal but bodily goods to consciously experienced goods.

McCormick, in defending this position, claims that "it seems very difficult to reject in vitro fertilization with embryo transfer in order to help a married couple otherwise childless achieve an ardently desired pregnancy on the sole ground of artificiality or of the separation of the unitive and procreative . . . unless one accepts this physically inseparability as an inviolable norm."[53] McCormick's claim here is akin to the claim that he and other dissenting theologians make in asserting that the Church's teaching on the wickedness of contraception is predicated upon a physicalism or biologism. In what follows I hope to show the reason why it is immoral and an irreverence for human life in its generation to choose to set aside the bond uniting marriage, marital coition, and the generation of human life by generating life in the laboratory. This reason is by no means rooted in the *physical inseparability* of the unitive and procreative meanings of the marital act. It is rather rooted in the intent to do evil by setting aside the great good of the maritally procreative act and substituting for it reproductive technologies.

D. Why It Is Morally Wicked and Irreverent to Human Life in Its Generation to Choose to Generate Human Life in the Laboratory

A useful way to begin this part of my analysis is to review briefly pertinent Church teaching on the subject. In 1949 Pope Pius XII, in rejecting artificial insemination by a husband, had this to say:

> We must never forget this: It is only the procreation of a new life according to the will and plan of the Creator which brings with it—to an astonishing degree of perfection—the realization of the desired ends. This is, at the same time, in harmony with the dignity of the marriage partners, with their bodily and spiritual natures, and with the normal and happy development of the child.[54]

Pius XII was evidently of the mind that God wills human life to be begotten *only* in the marital act (because he spoke of God's plan and will in the context of repudiating husband artificial insemination). He also indicated that this plan alone respected the dignity of husband and wife and their bodily-spiritual personhood and the dignity of the child as well.

In 1951 Pope Pius XII returned to this subject, one that obviously, because of the level of technological know-how, had not previously been of such concern as to warrant any consideration by the magisterium. In readdressing the subject Pope Pius XII then asserted:

> To reduce the cohabitation of married persons and the conjugal act to a mere organic function for the transmission of the germs of life would be to convert the domestic hearth, sanctuary of the family, into nothing more than a biological laboratory. . . . The conjugal act in its natural structure is a personal action, a simultaneous natural self-giving which, in the words of Holy Scripture, effects the union "in one flesh." This is more than the mere union of two germs, which can be brought about artificially—i.e., without the natural personal action of the spouses. The conjugal act as it is planned and willed by nature implies a *personal* cooperation [emphasis added], the right to which parties have mutually conferred on each other in contracting marriage.[55]

Here the Pontiff clearly indicates that the reason why human life ought to be given *only* in and through the marital act and *ought not* to be generated in the laboratory is that only in this way—one planned and willed by God—is it truly a *personal act* of the married couple, one to which they and they alone have a right. There is nothing physicalistic or biologistic about the thinking expressed here; it is rather a form of reasoning profoundly respectful of the personal and human significance of the act generating human life and of the personhood of both parents and child.

Although later pontiffs have not directly addressed the issue of the laboratory generation of human life, their teaching on marriage and its profoundly intimate and indispensable relationship to the reverential and responsible giving of human life clearly shows that they are of the same mind as Pius XII. Thus Pope Paul VI insisted that the Church had always taught as inviolable

> the inseparable connection, willed by God and unable to be broken by man on his own initiative, between the two meanings of the conjugal act: the unitive meaning and the procreative meaning. Indeed, by its intimate structure the conjugal act, while most closely uniting husband and wife, *capacitates them* [emphasis added] for the generation of new lives, according to laws inscribed in the very being of man and woman. By safeguarding both these essential aspects, the unitive and the procreative, the conjugal act preserves in its fullness the sense

of true mutual love and its ordination toward man's most high calling
to parenthood.[56]

It is most important to recognize that Pope Paul here insists that the conjugal act—the act in which husband and wife share their own persons and
their powers of genital sexuality with its love-giving and life-giving
dimensions—*capacitates* the spouses to generate new human life. He
recognized, of course, that nonmarried individuals have the physical power
to generate life, but his point is that only married persons in the very act
whereby they give themselves to each other in a bodily-spiritual communion are capable of giving human life *parentally*, i.e., in a responsible, loving, personal way. Again, there is nothing physicalistic or biologistic about
his line of reasoning.

Finally, Pope John Paul II, in his stirring homily on Washington's Mall,
insisted that human life is precious not only because it is a gift from a loving God but also because "it is the expression and the fruit of love." And
the love in question, he made clear in the context of his magnificent pro-
clamation of the gospel, is uniquely and specifically spousal, conjugal, marital
love. Continuing his remarks he said, "This is why life should spring up
within the setting of marriage."[57] Clearly he indicated here that the generation of human life ought only to be brought about within the covenant of
marital love. This theme, moreover, is one that crops up time and time again
in his series of addresses on the theology of the body.

Roman Catholic authors who justify in vitro fertilization for married
couples under the very limited condition already noted are, of course, aware
of these papal teachings. Still they claim that the insistence in these teachings on the *inviolability* of the bond between the unitive and procreative meanings of the marital act (and of the bond uniting marriage, the marital act,
and the generation of human life) is erroneous. McCormick suggests that
this insistence is predicated upon the belief that the choice to sunder this
bond is dehumanizing and immoral. But, he argues, this belief is in the nature
of an "intuition" and that other reasonable persons have different "intui-
tions" about the matter.[58] He further claims, as noted already, that the papal
teaching seems to erect the *phsycial inseparability* of the procreative and
unitive meanings of the conjugal act into a moral norm.

I think that we have sufficiently shown that this papal teaching is by
no means based on the physical inseparability of these meanings of the conjugal act but is rather rooted in a respect for the personal and human
significance of the conjugal act. I also believe that the teaching steadfastly
proposed by the Church, namely, that human life ought to be given *only*
in the conjugal act and *ought not* to be produced by the physical fusion of

male and female gametic cells in laboratories, is by no means the result of some unverifiable intuition. It is rather based on a clearheaded recognition of human, personal goods and the wickedness of deliberately choosing to set these goods aside.

The truth of this Church teaching can be made manifest, I think, by putting it in the form of a syllogism and then by showing the truth of the major and minor premises. The syllogism is the following:

> Any act of generating human life that is *nonmarital* is irresponsible because it is destructive of the great good of marriage and is also a violation of the reverence due to human life in its generation.

> But in vitro fertilization and other forms of the laboratory generation of human life, including vendor and husband artificial insemination, are nonmarital.

> Therefore these modes of generating human life are irresponsible.

In my opinion the minor premise of this argument does not require extensive discussion. Artificial insemination by a vendor is evidently nonmarital, and the same is obviously true of in vitro fertilization involving the use of ova and/or sperm from persons who are not married to each other. Moreover, husband artificial insemination and in vitro fertilization in which a wife's ovum is fertilized by sperm provided by her husband are likewise nonmarital in nature, even though married persons have collaborated in the procedure. Such procedures are nonmarital because they are *in principle* procedures that may be effected by persons who are not spouses; in addition and even more significantly, the spousal character of the man and woman participating in them is not *intrinsic to* the procedures themselves. What makes husband and wife capable of taking part in such forms of artful childmaking is *not* their being as spouses or their marriage but the simple fact that they produce gametic cells, ova in the case of the woman and sperm in the case of the man.

The major premise is the one that needs argument for its truth to become manifest. To show why this premise is true it is necessary, I believe, first to show why marriage, marital love, the marital act, and the parental generation of human life go together and then to show why the choice to engender human life nonmaritally is so destructive of goods crucial to human existence.

Since the intimate, personal, humanly significant bonds uniting marriage, marital love, the marital act and the parental generation of human life have been discussed at length in previous chapters, particularly in that on conjugal love, there is no need here to do more than summarize these points.

Let us therefore reflect briefly on the reasons why the marital act, and it alone, is a responsible procreative act. It is so because this is an act, first of all, that *only* spouses can choose. It is an act that only spouses can choose because only persons who have already given themselves to one another in the act of marital consent can collaborate in the marital act. Nonmarried persons can join their bodies in sexual coition, but what they choose to do is not the marital act but rather a simulation of it, a lie, for in choosing to copulate they do not unite irreplaceable persons but replaceable individuals.

The marital act, furthermore, is the only sort of act that spouses can choose if they are to exercise *maritally* their beautiful personal and sexual power of procreation, of giving life to a new human person. It is the only act in which the spouses personally share with each other their fertility and engage in an act open to the transmission of life.

The marital act, finally, is the only sort of act in which human life is begotten procreatively and responsibility. When human life is begotten in the sexual union of nonmarried persons, it is not begotten procreatively and responsibly because those begetting it cannot provide this irreplaceably precious human life with the home to which it has a right. When human life is begotten in the laboratory by use of gametic cells "provided" (by masturbation, remember, in the case of the male) by men and women who happen to be married, it is not generated in a procreative personal act of spouses but is rather generated by the *subsequent* activities of others (the doctors, etc.)

But why is the choice to sunder the bonds uniting marriage, marital love, the marital act, and the procreation of human life immoral? It is so for several reasons. First of all, it is immoral because it is in essence a choice that attacks the great good of marriage itself. We have already seen that the goods of marriage, martial love, and the procreative act go together. To attack one of these goods is to attack and do violence to the others. Our age sufficiently bears witness to the destruction done to the great human reality of marriage by denying the exclusive yet nonpossessive character of marital love, for we now have many who seriously, though foolishly, propose mate-swapping and "creative" adultery.[59] Our age likewise bears sufficient witness to the damage done to marriage by denying the goodness of marital procreativity, for many not only endorse the evils of contraception and abortion but also claim that married persons, by virtue of being spouses, do not have a right to procreate.[60] To choose to sever the bonds joining marriage, the marital act, and the generation of human life is further to threaten the good of marriage itself. Yet this is precisely what is being done when one adopts by free choice the proposal to generate human life in acts that are nonmarital in nature.

In addition, we must recognize that a human life, the life of a being that is the bearer of inviolable and inalienable rights, is not to be regarded as a product inferior in nature and subordinate in value to its "producers." Rather a human life is concretely an irreplaceable being of moral worth, a person, a being vicariously representing God Himself. The Christian, moreover, remembers that a human life, a human person, is a living word of God, of the God whose Uncreated Word became, for love of us, a created word. And the Uncreated Word who became and is still a created word, a fellow member of our species, is a Word that is, as we affirm in the Creed, "begotten, not made." Thus we, the created words of God, brothers and sisters of the eternally begotten Word of the Father, are to be begotten, not made. Human life, therefore, is to be begotten in and through the marital act, which is as it were a word spoken by husband and wife in which they affirm that they are open both to sharing life and love with each other and to sharing life and love with a new human life, a being who, like them, is irreplaceable and precious. It is therefore irresponsible and a grave violation of the reverence due to human life in its generation to choose to produce this life through the nonmarital act of fertilizing ova with sperm. Such an act may "make" a baby, and the baby[61] made by such an act is just as precious and irreplaceable as all other babies; yet such an act is not one of begetting human life procreatively.

To summarize: the choice to generate human life in the laboratory, insofar as it is the choice to generate human life nonmaritally, is wicked and irresponsible because it is a choice that threatens the good of marriage itself and by so doing endangers human life in its generation. It is likewise wicked because it is a choice that violates the reverence due human life in its generation insofar as it transforms the act of begetting human life from one of procreative marital love to one of artistic production, thereby treating human life not as a good of incomparable and priceless value but rather as a product subordinate to its producers.

The desire of couples childless because of infertility or blocked fallopian tubes is in itself a noble desire. But the moral question centers not on this desire but on the human deeds freely chosen in order to satisfy it. A personalistic human ethics is just as much concerned with means as it is with ends, for we can, unfortunately, choose to do some dreadful deeds with the best of motives and with the noblest of ends in view.

Moreover, married couples who cannot have a child because of blocked fallopian tubes (the usual reason for resorting to in vitro fertilization) can be helped in other ways. Surgical reconstruction of the fallopian tubes is currently possible in approximately thirty percent of cases—a far higher succes rate than efforts to "produce" children through in vitro fertilization. Moreover, it has been suggested that it may be possible to remove the ovum from the ovaries, implant it in the fallopian tubes below the point where the tube is blocked, and then have husband and wife unite in the act of marital love.[62] This procedure, should it prove workable, is in my judgment morally permissible, and offers great hope for those married couples for whom the laboratory generation of human life is now proposed.[63]

To conclude this part of this chapter. Human life is to be begotten, not made. It is beggoten in the marital act, it is made through the various forms of artful childmaking. To resort to such procedures, then, is wrong not because of any physicalistic or biologistic taboo but because it is destructive of human persons and the goods meant to flourish within them.

2. The Infamy of Abortion and the Need to Protect Human Life in Its Generation by Just Laws

The Church has constantly taught throughout its history that abortion is a terrible evil, a criminal attack upon human life.[64] The gravest irreverence to human life in its generation is to kill it.

The mind of the Church on this question is so well known that it is difficult to imagine how anyone could be ignorant of it. Yet this teaching, a truly liberating truth, is frequently caricatured, even by some Catholics, as a repressive taboo. It may be well, then, in this brief consideration of abortion, to recall to mind the teaching of the Church, for in doing so it will become evident that this teaching is predicated upon the dignity and sanctity of human life and the irreplaceable value of the human person.

Pius XII eloquently expressed the mind of the Church on this matter when he said:

> . . . the baby in the mother's womb has the right to life immediately from God. Hence there is no man, no human authority, no science, no medical, eugenic, social, economic or moral "indication" which can establish or grant a valid judicial ground for a direct deliberate disposition of an innocent human life, that is, a disposition which looks to its destruction either as an end or as a means to another end perhaps just in itself. The baby, still not born, is a man in the same degree and for the same reasons as the mother.[65]

The Fathers of Vatican Council II were firm in their absolute rejection of abortion as an infamous crime. They wrote:

Whatever is opposed to life itself, such as any type of murder, genocide, abortion, euthanasia, or wilful self-destruction . . . are infamies indeed. They poison human society, but they do more harm to those who practice them than those who suffer from the injury.[66]

God, the Lord of life, has conferred on men the surpassing ministry of safeguarding life—a ministry which must be fulfilled in a manner which is worthy of man. Therefore, from the moment of its conception life must be guarded with the greatest care, while abortion and infanticide are unspeakable crimes.[67]

Pope Paul VI clearly taught the evil of abortion, affirming that "the direct interruption of generation already begun, and especially direct abortion . . . must be entirely repudiated."[68] Finally, in his homily on the Mall Pope John Paul II valiantly upheld the sacred dignity of unborn human life, declaring, "When the sacredness of life before birth is attacked, we will stand up and proclaim that no one ever has the authority to destroy unborn human life."[69]

Abortion is the greatest violation of human life in its generation because it is the wilful destruction of this life during the period of its development when it is most defenseless and helpless. That abortion is the destruction of a human being with potential and not of a merely potential human being[70] cannot reasonably be denied today in terms of what we know about the significance of conception/fertilization. Here the comments of Professor C.G. Goodhart of the zoology department at Cambridge University are pertinent. Professor Goodhart was responding to the claim made by Malcolm Potts, a biologist strongly in support of abortion, that no one can tell when a new human individual comes into being. In his response Goodhart said:

Dr. Potts has argued that human development is a continuous process . . . and that it is in principle impossible to define when a new human individual comes into existence. May I with great respect suggest that this is a view which is contradicted by biological knowledge? For there is a real discontinuity at fertilization, or to be pedantic, at the "activation" of the ovum, which is not necessarily always the same thing. This is the point after, but not before, it becomes capable of completing its development without any further stimulus from outside. Once activated, the organism will continue its development until it dies. That is what most of us would have called the moment of conception, however else the British Council of Churches [or the Supreme Court] may now have decided to define the word. But whatever we call it, it occurs at a specific point in time, after, but not before which, development can proceed; and that is a real *discontinuity* marking the coming into existence of a new biological organism [in the case of humans, a new human life].[71]

Although some writers, including Charles E. Curran,[72] allege that the phenomenon of twinning and the possibility of recombination[73] refute the view than an individual human life is present at conception/fertilization (or "activation," to use Goodhart's language), this allegation cannot stand. As Benedict Ashley, O.P. and others[74] have clearly shown, twinning is not incompatible with individual human life at conception/fertilization insofar as twinning can be reasonably explained as a kind of natural "cloning." From *one already existing* human being another is derived by a process, still not fully understood, of asexual generation. Recombination of two or more individuals (conceived by the fertilization of several ova by different sperm) in humans has never been shown to occur and, as Thomas Hilgers, M.D., demonstrates, is not possible in human gestation because of the protection provided the developing human life by the *zona pellucida* surrounding it.[75]

The basic reason why many in our culture accept abortion is their dualism and their consequentialism. Faced with the massive biological evidence that a new human life indeed comes into existence at fertilization, they sharply distinguish between human beings who are biologically alive and those who are "meaningfully" or "personally" alive. The dualistic presupposition behind their justification of abortion has been accurately stated by Michael Tooley (who agrees with this presupposition), who said, "membership in a species is of no moral significance."[76] What this means is that it is not of central moral significance that a living being is member of the human species. Simply being a human being is not, of itself, sufficient to make the human being a being of moral worth, a bearer of inalienable and inviolable rights. If, however, being a human being is not sufficient, what is? Here the supporters of abortion have insurmountable difficulty in agreeing among themselves. Some, like the Supreme Court justices, would make being born the crucially important factor. Others, like Daniel Callahan, would contend that only those human beings with "a developed capacity for reasoning, willing, desiring, and relating to others"[77] are "meaningfully alive," whereas still others argue that a certain level of I.Q. is necessary.[78] In reality all who distinguish between those human beings who are merely biologically alive and those who are "meaningfully" or "personally" alive are dualists, for they deny that a living human body is a person and deny that membership in the human species of transcendent importance.

As we have seen repeatedly in this work, a dualistic conception of the human person goes hand in glove with a consequentialistic, quality of life ethic. For the defenders of abortion will even argue that if one grants that a human unborn baby is, at least at some stage in its development, "meaningfully" or "personally" alive (and some defenders of directly intended abortion, e.g. Charles E. Curran and Richard A. McCormick[79] will grant this), it is still morally choiceworthy to kill it if the choice to kill can be justified by some "proportionately greater good."

This mentality, one that we have encountered frequently enough throughout this work is a specious personalism. The Church's firm defense of the unborn child's right to life is, like its firm repudiation of contraception, sterilization, and the manufacturing of life in the laboratory, an authentic personalism that refuses to repudiate the bodily character of human existence and of human personhood. Every living human body, every living member of the human species, is a person and a bearer of inviolable rights that must be recognized and protected by society. This is the firm, clear, and liberating truth that the Church proclaims, especially in defending the lives of the unborn.

This teaching, moreover, is crucial to human civilization. As Ramsey noted, it is a teaching "so fundamental to the edifice of Western law and morals that it cannot be removed without bringing the whole house down."[80] This truth can perhaps be made even more evident if we reflect briefly on some critically important remarks of the philosopher Mortimer Adler. Adler defended the view that membership in the human species is of critical moral significance because the human animal is an animal radically different in kind from other kinds of animals—the human animal alone is a *person* and not a thing. In arguing for the truth of this claim, Adler noted that if one denies that *being a human being* is of moral significance, then

> those who now oppose injurious discrimination on the moral ground that all human beings, being equal in their humanity, should be treated equally in all those respects that concern their common humanity, would have no solid basis in fact to support their normative principle. A social and political ideal that has operated with revolutionary force in human history could be validly dismissed as a hollow illusion that should become defunct. . . . We can now imagine a future state of affairs in which a new global division of mankind replaces all old parochial divisions based upon race, nationality, or ethnic group. . . . a division that separates the human elite at the top of the scale from the human scum at the bottom, a division based on accurate scientific measurements of human ability and achievement and one, therefore, that is factually incontrovertible.[81]

The legalization of abortion, which denies to the unborn their status as beings of moral worth by reason of their humanity, includes them among the scum. But it not only places them in this terrible position, it likewise poses a threat to many others. For we now live in a society where the criterion for equal protection of the law against homicide is no longer one's humanity but one's "quality of life" or the "meaningfulness" of one's life. We are beginning to see newborn children denied common medical treatment, and it is no doubt true that many elderly and handicapped persons are likewise being denied the care to which they are entitled. It is thus absolutely mandatory to restore the protection of law to the unborn.

The liberating truth of the Church's teaching on abortion, as well as its teaching on sexual morality and marriage, must be made known once more to people of our culture. For this teaching alone respects human persons, male and female, born and unborn, young and old, healthy and crippled. For it is only by revering human life in its generation that we will be able properly to revere it in its being.

NOTES

[1] Pope John Paul II, " 'Stand Up' for Human Life," *Origins: NC Documentary Service* 9.18 (October 18, 1979) 279.

[2] See *Yes to Life*, edited by the Daughters of St. Paul (Boston: St. Paul Editions, 1977). This is an excellent collection of source material from the *Didache* to the 1976 Pastoral Letter of the American Hierarchy, *To Live in Christ Jesus*, bringing together the consistent teaching of the Church on the reverence due to life and the sacredness of life.

[3] See, for example, *Gaudium et Spes*, nn. 26, 27.

[4] I wish to note here that I am not claiming that an *is* (the fact that a human being is a being of moral worth) of itself grounds an *ought* (the obligation to respect and reverence human life). The basis for our moral obligation to respect and reverence human life is the intelligent directive of practical reasonableness (i.e., a basic principle of morality) that we are to do good and avoid evil and that life itself is a good of persons. On this matter see Thomas Aquinas, *Summa Theologiae*, 1-2, 94, 2.

[5] Pope John Paul II, "An Address to the U.S. Bishops" (October 5, 1979), *Origins* 9.18 (October 18, 1979) 289.

[6] Paul Ramsey, *Ethics at the Edges of Life: Medical and Legal Intersections* (New Haven: Yale University Press, 1978), p. xiv.

[7] On the knowability of this, see Mortimer Adler, *The Difference of Man and the Difference It Makes* (New York: Meridian, 1968).

[8] *California Medicine*, "A New Ethic for Medicine and Society," September, 1970, 67-68.

⁹ These notions of human life are contradictory inasmuch as the one affirms what the other denies and vice versa. Since these notions are truly contradictory, and not merely contrary, one must be true and the other must be false.

¹⁰ John Courtney Murray, S.J., *We Hold These Truths: Catholic Reflections on the American Proposition* (New York: Sheed and Ward, 1960), p. 45.

¹¹ Among Roman Catholic theologians who hold that not all members of the human species are subjects of protectable rights but that some, for instance fetal human beings, are merely biologically alive and only "on their way to personhood" are Daniel C. Maguire and Daniel Callahan. For Maguire, see his *Death by Choice* (New York: Doubleday, 19 74), pp. 199-202 (cf. pp. 7, 12-13) and also his *The Moral Choice* (New York: Doubleday, 1978), p. 448. For Callahan see his *Abortion: Law, Choice and Morality* (New York: Macmillan, 1970).

Among Roman Catholics who accept the proposition that it is sometimes right deliberately and of set purpose to do evil so that good may come about are Joseph Fuchs, Bruno Sch¼uller, Louis Janssens, John Dedek, Charles E. Curran, Richard A. McCormick, Philip S. Keane, Timothy E. O'Connell. For the abundant literature demonstrating this see Richard A. McCormick, *Notes on Moral Theology 1965-1980* (Washington: University Press of America, 1981) and Timothy E. O'Connell, *Principles for a Catholic Morality* (New York: Seabury, 1978). For essays criticizing these views see those compiled in *Principles of Catholic Moral Life*, edited by William E. May (Chicago: Franciscan Herald Press, 1981).

¹² This proposition, which is latent in many if not most arguments to support abortion, the "benign neglect" of "defective" children, and mercy killing, is formally articulated by Michael Tooley, "Abortion and Infanticide," *Philosophy and Public Affairs 2* (Fall, 1972) 37-65.

¹³ This proposal is simply a way of saying that the end justifies the means. See the literature cited in note 11.

¹⁴ Christian writers, including Pope Paul VI in *Humanae Vitae*, have consistently seen in Romans 3.8 the revealed source for the principle that we are not to do evil for the sake of good to come. For an incisive critique of the revisionist views of proportionalist Catholic theologians, who render this advice of St. Paul nugatory or banal, see John M. Finnis, "The Natural Law, Objective Morality, and Vatican Council II," in *Principles of Catholic Moral Life* pp. 113-150. Germain G. Grisez, *The Way of Our Lord Jesus Christ*, Vol. 1, *Christian Moral Principles* (Chicago: Franciscan Herald Press, 1983), Ch. 6.

¹⁵ The term "practical reasonableness" if used by Finnis in his *Natural Law and Natural Rights* (Oxford: Clarendon Law Series, Oxford University Press, 1980) and by Germain Grisez in many of his writings, cf. his *Abortion: The Myths, the Realities, and the Arguments* (New York: Corpus, 1970) as a synonym for natural law.

¹⁶ On basic principles or precepts of practical reasonableness (the natural law), see Thomas Aquinas, *Summa Theologiae* 1-2, 91, 2; 94, 2. On this matter see

Finnis, *Natural Law and Natural Rights*, pp. 59-133.

[17] On the self-evident character of the basic precepts of practical reasonableness see Thomas Aquinas, *Summa Theologiae*, 1-2, 94, 2. See also Germain G. Grisez, "The First Principle of Practical Reason: A Commentary on the *Summa Theologiae*, 1a2ae, 94, 2" *Natural Law Forum* 10 (1965) 168-196 (reprinted in abridged form in *Aquinas: A Collection of Critical Essays*, edited by Antony Kenny. New York: Doubleday Anchor, 1969, pp. 430-483). Also see R. H. Armstrong, *The Primary and Secondary Precepts in Thomistic Natural Law Teaching* (The Hague: Martinus Nijhoff, 1965).

[18] The best contemporary works showing why this is true are those of Finnis and Grisez already cited. See also Germain G. Grisez and Joseph M. Boyle, Jr., *Life and Death With Liberty and Justice: A Contribution to the Euthanasia Debate* (Notre Dame, In.: University of Notre Dame Press, 1978), Chapter Eleven.

[19] See Murray, *We Hold These Truths*, pp. 45-50.

[20] *Dignitatis Humanae*, n. 3.

[21] On this see Grisez and Boyle, *Life and Death With Liberty and Justice*, pp. 240-58, 298-335.

[22] Pope John Paul II, " 'Stand Up' For Human Life," 279.

[23] Unfortunately, as mentioned in the text later, many today seek to avoid this tragedy by resorting to contraceptives, backed up by abortion. On the folly of this approach see James M. Ford, M.D., and Michael Schwartz, "Birth Control for Teenagers: Diagram for Disaster," *Linacre Quarterly* 46.1 (February, 1979) 71-81.

[24] Pope John Paul II, " 'Stand Up' For Human Life," 279.

[25] On this see K. D. Whitehead, *Agenda for the Sexual Revolution: Abortion, Contraception, Sex Education and Related Evils* (Chicago: Franciscan Herald Press, 1981), pp. 101-117.

[26] For proposals of this sort, see the work by the former Catholic priest, Robert Francoeur, *Utopian Motherhood* (New York: Doubleday, 1970).

[27] I use this term advisedly. In his article, "Artificial Insemination: Beyond the Best Interests of the Donor," *Hastings Center Report* 9.4 (August, 1979) 14-15, 43, lawyer George J. Annas noted that the term "donor" is a misnomer and that those males who provide sperm for artificial insemination by women whom they do not even know should better be termed "sperm vendors." He wrote: "It is a contract in which the vendor is agreeing to do certain things for pay. . . . The continued use of the term 'donor' gives the impression that the sperm vendor is doing some service for the good of humanity," and this is an erroneous impression.

[28] Cloning, also known as nuclear transplantation, is a mode of generating life that is asexual insofar as it does not require the union of male and female gametic cells. In cloning the nucleus of an unfertilizad ovum is destroyed by radiation and replaced by the nucleus of a cell taken from the body of another individual. The ovum then has a full set of chromosomes and acts as if it had

been fertilized. The resulting individual is a twin or carbon copy of the individual whose body cell was used to renucleate the ovum.

[29] Pope Paul VI, *Humanae Vitae*, n. 12.

[30] The expression "artful childmaking" is suggested by the title of a work by John Wakefield, *Artful Childmaking* (St. Louis: Pope John XXIII Medical-Moral Reserach Center, 1978).

[31] Richard A. McCormick, *How Brave a New World? Dilemmas in Bioethics* (New York: Doubleday, 1981), pp. 308-312.

[32] *Ibid.*, pp. 309-311.

[33] Joseph F. Fletcher, "Ethical Aspects of Genetic Controls: Designed Genetic Changes in Man," *New England Journal of Medicine* 285 (1971) 776-783; Robert Francoeur, *Utopian Motherhood: New Trends in Human Reproduction* (New York: Doubleday, 1970); Michael Hamilton, "New Life for Old: Genetic Decisions," *Christian Century* 86 (19609) 74.

[34] Fletcher, "Ethical Aspects of Genetic Controls," 781-782.

[35] This is the subtitle Fletcher gave to his book, *The Ethics of Genetic Control: Ending Reproductive Roulette* (New York: Doubleday 1974).

[36] On this see Nicholas Crotty, "The Technological Imperative: Reflection on Reflections," *Theological Studies* 33.3 (September, 1972) 441-447.

[37] On this it is instructive to read Thomas Aquinas, *In Decem Libros Ethicorum Aristotelis Expositio* (Rome, Marietti, 1955) Liber I, lectio 1, n. 2.

[38] Ashley Montagu, *Sex, Man and Culture* (Philadelphia: Lippincott, 1969), pp. 13-14.

[39] McCormick confuses matter, in my judgment by using "consequentialist" and "teleological" as synonyms. A teleological ethical theory, as opposed to a formalistic, duty oriented deontological theory, need not be consequentialistic. For a good presentation of this matter see Grisez and Boyle, *Life and Death With Liberty and Justice*, pp. 345-361. See also Frederick S. Carney, "On McCormick and Teleological Morality," *Journal of Religious Ethics* 6 (Spring, 1978) 81-107.

[40] McCormick, *How Brave a New World?* p. 311.

[41] *Ibid.*, p. 312.

[42] Johannes Gründel, "Zeugung in der Retorte-unsittlich?" *Stimmen der Zeit* 103 (1978) 675-682; Charles E. Curran, *Politics, Medicine, and Christian Ethics: Dialogue with Paul Ramsey* (Philadelphia: Fortress Press, 1973), pp. 200-219; McCormick, *How Brave a New World?.*, pp. 306-325.

[43] Leon Kass, "Making Babies: The New Biology and the 'Old' Moralty," *The Public Interest* 26 (Winter), 1972) 28-56; Kass, "Babies by Means of *In Vitro* Fertilization: Unethical Experiment on the Unborn?" *New England Journal of Medicine* 285 (1971) 1174-1179; Paul Ramsey, "Shall We 'Reproduce'? I. The Medical Ethics of *In Vitro* Fertilization," *Journal of the American Medical Association* 220 (1972) 1346-1350; Ramsey, "Shall We 'Reproduce'? II. Rejoinders and Future Forecast," *Journal of the American Medical Association* 220 (1972) 1480-1485). Kass later returned to this subject in his "Making Babies'

Revisited," *The Public Interest* 54 (Winter, 1979) 32-59. In his more recent article Kass, while still arguing against in vitro fertilization, suggests that the risk of harm need not be positively excluded. It is sufficient if it is equivalent to or less than the risks to the child from normal procreation.

[44] Ramsey, "Shall We 'Reproduce'? I," 1347.

[45] *Ibid.*

[46] *Ibid.*

[47] See, for instance, Curran, *Politics, Medicine, and Christian Ethics*, p. 212.

[48] McCormick, *How Brave a New World?*, p. 331.

[49] For an extensive survey of the literature on this see Le Roy Walters, "Human In Vitro Fertilization: A Review of the Literature," *Hastings Center Report* 9.4 (August, 1979) 23-43, especially p. 27 for the scientific literature.

[50] McCormick, *How Brave a New World?* p. 332.

[51] See above, Chapter Five, Section II.

[52] On this matter see Finnis, *Natural Law and Natural Rights*, pp. 223-226.

[53] McCormick, *How Brave a New World?*, pp. 328-329.

[54] Pope Pius XII, "To Catholic Doctors: An Address by His Holiness to the Fourth International Convention of Catholic Doctors, Castelgondolfo, Italy, September 29, 1949," *The Catholic Mind* 48 (1950) 250-253.

[55] Pope Pius XII, "Apostolate of the Midwives: An Address by His Holiness to the Italian Catholic Union of Midwives, October 29, 1951," *The Catholic Mind* 50 (1952) 61.

[56] Pope Paul VI, *Humanae Vitae*, n. 12.

[57] Pope John Paul II, " 'Stand Up' For Human Life," 279.

[58] McCormick, *How Brave a New World?*, p. 328.

[59] See, for instance, Robert and Anna Francoeur's advocacy of such creative adultery in their "The Technology of Man-Made Sex," in *The Future of Sexual Relations* (Englewood Cliffs, N.J.: Prentice-Hall, 1973). See also the views of Anthony Kosnik et al., *Human Sexuality: New Directions in American Catholic Thought* (New York: Paulist Press, 1977), pp. 148-149.

[60] For instance, Joseph F. Fletcher in his *The Ethics of Genetic Control*.

[61] Here it is important to note the revealing, if inadvertent, remark made by Dr. Robert Edwards (One of the doctors involved in the laboratory generation of Louise Brown): "The last time I saw *her, she* was just eight cells in a test tube. *She* was beautiful *then*, and she's still beautiful *now*." *Science Digest*, October, 1978, 9; emphasis added. Surely this is eloquent testimony that human life begins at fertilization.

[62] I have been informed that this may be a very realistic possiblilty by Dr. Joseph Ricotta, an eminent Catholic gynecologist in Buffalo, New York.

[63] I must note here that should the procedure become possible, one would first have to meet conditions regarding risks to the child conceived. There would not, in this instance, be any experimentation on human life in the laboratory; nevertheless, studies in animals should precede any application to humans in order to determine whether this procedure might itself cause harm to progeny.

⁶⁴ A good study to show this is that of John R. Connery, *Abortion: The Development of the Roman Catholic Perspective* (Chicago: Loyola University Press, 1977).

⁶⁵ Pope Pius XII, *Acta Apostolicae Sedis* 43 (1951) 838-839.

⁶⁶ *Gaudium et Spes*, n. 27.

⁶⁷ Ibid., n. 51.

⁶⁸ Pope Paul VI, *Humanae Vitae*, n. 14.

⁶⁹ Pope John Paul II, " 'Stand Up' for Human Life," 280.

⁷⁰ An excellent philosophical demonstration of the personhood of the unborn is that of Robert Joyce, "When Does a Person Begin?" in *New Perspectives on Human Abortion*, edited by Thomas Hilgers, M.D., Dennis J. Horan, and David Mall (Frederick, Md.: University Publications of America, 1981), pp. 345-356.

⁷¹ C. B. Goodhart, "Reply to Dr. Potts," in *Biology and Ethics*, edited by F. C. Ebeling (New York/London: Academic Press, 1969), pp. 101-103.

⁷² Curran, *Politics, Medicine, and Christian Ethics*, pp. 115-119.

⁷³ Recombination, or the combining of several individuals into one, has been achieved in the laboratory in work on mice.

⁷⁴ Benedict Ahsley, O.P., "A Critique of the Theory of Delayed Hominization,' in *An Ethical Evaluation of Fetal Experimentation: An Interdisciplinary Study*, edited by Donald G. McCarthy and Albert S. Morazewski, O.P. (St. Louis: Pope John XXIII Medical-Moral Research Center, 1976, pp. 113-135.

⁷⁵ Thomas Hilgers, M.D., "Human Reproduction: Three Issues for the Moral Theologian," *Theological Studies* 38.1 (March, 1977) 136-152.

⁷⁶ Tooley, "Abortion and Infanticide," 44.

⁷⁷ Callahan, *Abortion: Law, Choice and Morality*, p. 378.

⁷⁸ Fletcher, for instance, postulates an I.Q. of at least 20 and more probably of at least 40 in order for an individual human being to count as a person. See his "Indicators of Humanhood: A Tentative Profile of Man," in *Hastings Center Report* 2.5 (November, 1972) 1-4.

⁷⁹ Curran and McCormick both hold that after implantation there is truly individual human life present. For Curran see his *Politics, Medicine and Ethics*, pp. 115-119; for McCormick see *How Brave a New World?*, pp. 191-206.

⁸⁰ Ramsey, *Ethics at the Edges of Life*, p. xiv.

⁸¹ Adler, *The Difference of Man and the Difference It Makes* pp. 264-265.

Index

The publication of this book was made possible in part through the support of the Christendom Publishing Group. Members are listed below:

Sister Ellen S.J.W.
Mr & Mrs Howard A. Baizaire
Mrs. Marie Barrett
Mr. Joseph C. Berzanskis
Mr. John F. Bradley
Reverend Nicholas Brennan
Mr. & Mrs. Robert Brindle
Mrs. Martha Brown
Mr. James G. Bruen Jr.
Deacon Patrick Bruen
Mr. & Mrs. Merv Burns
Paul A. Busam M.D.
Mrs. Marie Butkus
Mrs. Margaret Buytaert
Miss Priscilla Carmody
Mrs. Virginia J. Chipp
Mr. Eugene V. Clark
Mr. & Mrs. Christopher Colclough
Mrs. S. J. Conner
Mr. John W.W. Cooper
Mrs. Marie A. Cooper
Mr. Terence J. Coyne
CH (Maj) Alfred M. Croke
Mr. & Mrs. Chris N. Cuddeback
Mrs. Ellen L. Dalby
Mrs. Jack Deardurff
Reverend Robert J. Dempsey
Reverend Daniel B. Dixon
Mr. Thomas C. Domeika
Mr. & Mrs. Leon W. Doty
Mr. John H. Duffy
Mrs. James Ebben
Mr. D. N. Ehart
Mr. Clinton M. Elges
Mr. William W. Elliott
Mrs. Betty Emilio
Reverend George S. Endal S.J.

Mr. Francis G. Fanning
Mr. & Mrs. Victor Fernandez
Mr. & Mrs. James G. Fischer
Miss Margaret C. Fitzgerald
G. F. Flagg Family
Mr. Eugene P. Foeckler Sr.
Mr. John F, Foell
Mr. & Mrs. J. P. Frank Jr.
Mrs. Adele Fricke
Mr. Eduardo Garcia-Ferrer
Mr. & Mrs. John Gardner
Mr. Richard L. Gerhards
Mr. Patrick Guinan
Mrs. Paula Haigh
Mr. Robert E. Hanna
Mr. Frank E. Hauck
Mr. David Havlicek
Mr. Ronald H. Herrmann
Mr. Larry L. Hobbs
Mr. & Mrs. Andre Huck
Mrs. Doris L. Huff
Edgar Hull M.D.
Mrs. Carmen Iacobelli
Mr. & Mrs. Dave Jaszkowiak
Mr. Bruce Jones
Mrs. Kathleen C. Jones
Mr. Marley Francis Jones
Mr. Edward E. Judge
Mrs. J. M. Keiper
Reverend Michael J. Kelly
Mr. & Mrs. Frank Knoell
Mr. John R. Knoll
James W. Lassiter M.D.
Miss Therese Lawrence
Mr. Edward A. Lewandowski
Very Rev. Victor O. Lorenz
Mr. William J. Lucas

Members of the Christendom Publishing Group, continued

Jackie Luebbert
Mrs. Carolyn C. MacDonald
Mr. George F. Manhardt
Mr. Thomas Manning
Miss Jeanette Maschmann
N. Anthony Mastropietro M.D.
Reverend Mark G. Mazza
Mr. Thomas J. McCann
Reverend William R. McCarthy
Mr. John A. McCarty Esq.
Mrs. Miriam McCue
Mr. Joseph D. McDaid
Mrs. John (Sandra) McDevitt
Mr. & Mrs. Dennis P. McEneany
Mr. J. R. McMahon
Mrs. Kenneth McNichol
Patrick A. Metress
Mr. & Mrs. Larry Miggins
Mr. Joseph Monahan
Reverend Hugh Monmonier
Mr. James B. Mooney
Mrs. Gertrude G. Moore
Mr. Nicholas J. Mulhall
Mr. & Mrs. G. W. Muth
Mr. L. Maxwell Narby
Mr. Frank C. Nelick
Mr. Frank Newlin
Maj. Michael J. O'Hara USMC
Mr. Chris T. O'Keefe
Mr. John F. O'Shaughnessy Jr.
Miss Veronica M. Oravec
Mrs. John F. Parker
Mr. Ernest Patry
Reverend Angelo Patti
Brother Stephen F. Paul
Rev. Mr. Laszlo S. Pavel
Bill and Mary Peffley

Mr. Alfred H. Pekarek
Robert N. Pelaez M.D.
Mrs. Angela M. Peters
Mr. & Mrs. Pat Pollock
Mr. & Mrs. William H. Power Jr.
Mr. Stuart Quinlan
Mrs. Mary F. Quinn
Mr. Thomas J. Quinn
Mr. & Mrs. Joseph E. Rau
Reverend Robert A. Reed
Mrs. John F. Reid
Mr. & Mrs. John J. Reuter
Msgr. William J. Reynolds
Dr. & Mrs. Robert C. Rice
M. V. Rock M.D.
Brother Philip Romano OFMCap
Mrs. Paul Rosenberger
Mr. Bernard J. Ruby
Mr. Mark V. Ruessmann
Mr. Richard W. Sassman
Mr. Edward F. Scanlon
Mr. & Mrs. George Scanlon
Miss Marian C. Schatzman
Mrs. Margaret Scheetz
Mr. Peter Scheetz
Miss Constance M. Scheez
Mrs. Francis R. Schirra
Mrs. Claragene Schmidt
John B. Shea
John R. Sheehan M.D.
Miss Anne Sherman
Mrs. Bernice Simon
Mr. Richard M. Sinclair Jr.
Capt. Arthur Sippo
Mrs. Walter Skorupski
Mrs. Joan M. Smith
Mrs. Mary Carole Smith

Members of the Christendom Publishing Group, continued

Mr. William Smith
Mr. & Mrs. James Spargo
Mr. Michael Sullivan
Mr. John Svarc
Mr. Edward S. Szymanski
Ms. C. G. Teixeira
Mr. Edward B. Timko
Mr. Richard J. Titus
Mr. Dominic Torlone
Rev. Chris Twohig
Mr. Michael Vachon
Mr. & Mrs. Albert Vallone
Mr. Willem Van Achthoven
Mrs. Alice Vandenberg
Reverend Frederick J. Vaughn
Mr. William C. Vinet Jr.
Mrs. Catherine Wahlmeier
Mr. David P. Walkey
Mrs. Alice V. Ward
Mr. Fulton John Waterloo
Mr. Ralph A. Wellings
Mr. Alfred L. White
Miss Penny Wiest
Mr. John R. Wilhelmy
Mrs. Mary Williams
Mr. Michael C. Winn
Mrs. Marguerite A. Wright
James F. Zimmer M.D.